THE CHALLENGE OF ISLAM

C.R.Marsh

ARK PUBLISHING
130 City Road, London EC1V 2NJ

© Charles Marsh 1980
First published 1980, by Ark Publishing,
130 City Road, London EC1V 2NJ.

ISBN 0 86201 082 9

Typesetting by Nuprint Services Ltd, Harpenden, Herts
Printed in England by McCorquodale (Newton) Ltd.,
Newton-le-Willows, Lancashire.

Contents

Introduction

Make Jesus King was the motto chosen by a company of young Christian students in their eagerness to evangelise the whole world. It was a misleading watchword, for God has assured us in his Word of the ultimate and final triumph of the Lord Jesus Christ. 'Jesus shall reign' is not mere wishful thinking. 'I have set my King upon Zion, my holy hill' is the solemn declaration of God.

Within a few days, Muslim students in North Africa cabled the challenging reply, 'Islam defies your King'. The words imply: 'Wherever else your Lord may triumph, it shall never be in Muslim lands.' This is the attitude of every Muslim to our wonderful Lord, and if you are a committed Christian it will come as a personal challenge to *you*. This book is an attempt to show how we have tried, for the past fifty years, to meet the challenge and encourage young Christians to face it in the power of the Holy Spirit.

A rapid world survey shows that it is a very real challenge. At Bethlehem, where our Lord was born, the call to prayer rings out from the minarets five times a day, 'God is greater. There is no God but Allah, and Mohammed is his Apostle.' Mohammed has superseded Christ. At Mecca, where Mohammed was born, no Christian has ever dared to preach the gospel openly.

A few years ago Islam was regarded as a dying religion, but today it claims more than 600,000,000 followers throughout the world. The vast majority of Christian missionaries have been expelled from Muslim lands. Cash from the sale of Arabian oil is being used to build magnificent mosques throughout the world. The presence of 8,000,000 Muslims in Europe constitutes an additional challenge. Islam has gone over to the attack. Muslims plan to build a mosque in every major town in Great Britain, and to reach every family in door-to-door visitation.

This book tells of our early experiences in Algeria. During the past few years, God in his wonderful grace has given me a totally new ministry. In some ways it has been the outstanding miracle of my life—to be able to relate to European students. This has meant a complete reorientation of my thinking, enabling me to transfer from the mentality of a Muslim society to a virtually pagan content. It has taken place by learning to listen to young people, to sympathise with them, to reorientate my thinking; and all this has been motivated by a sincere love for my Lord and a deep concern for the young. I firmly believe that this would have been impossible on my own, but a simple dependence on the renewing power of the Holy Spirit has brought about a transformation. If it is possible for an old man of over seventy to switch from Muslim mentality to that of present day youth, surely the converse can take place in young Christians who are willing to endeavour to think as Muslims do, as the first step to their evangelisation. May the Lord use this book to lead you to a deeper understanding of Islam, and bring you to the conviction that the evangelisation of the Muslim world is priority number one in our day and generation.

Chapter One

The Call and Preparation

Fifty-eight years ago, just after the First World War, I was working on a farm in Kent. After a hard day's work I was enjoying a good wash in the bedroom of the house where I was lodging. Suddenly I heard a voice ring out, 'Prepare to meet thy God.' The speaker went on to preach the gospel.

I flung up the old-fashioned window sash and leaned out. In front of the village pub one hundred yards away stood a lone sailor. It was evident that he had walked out from Chatham dockyard and was spending his day's leave in going from village to village preaching. Such is the ardour of youth! It was just one month after my conversion, but as I listened I realised that this young man had passed through an experience similar to my own. He had found new life in Christ, and wanted to share the wonderful thrill of sins forgiven and this fantastic experience of coming to know God personally. What a challenge it presented to me as a young Christian! Surely I could not leave him to stand there alone? I did not know the first thing about preaching, but I could just stand with him and perhaps hold his hat. I finished washing, put on my jacket and went out and stood behind him as he faced the pub.

He could not see his audience, but they were there inside, drinking and joking. The sailor was a stranger to me and to them, but I was well known. To my left was the old wooden house where I had previously rented a room for four months. The ceiling was so low that I could not stand upright. The girl of the house was sleeping with another lodger, and although unmarried was expecting a child. Every evening they had gambled, smoked and drunk. Behind me was the church which I had attended until my conversion, in spite of the fact that the rector quite obviously never prepared his sermons. Opposite the church was the Colporter's house. He was known locally as the 'Bible Puncher'. He trundled round the villages with the help of his old-fashioned tricycle. Had he been at home he would most certainly have stood with us. Just down the road was the blacksmith's shop. I had good cause to remember that shop, as he was also the wheelwright; and the week before I had been sent with a frisky pony to take back to the farm the newly painted pony trap. I had been all out for speed, and flicked the pony with the whip. She had responded by kicking up her heels and smashing the front of the trap. Very shamefacedly I had to take the broken trap back to be re-repaired. Yes, they all knew me in that village—a bit of a greenhorn, slightly religious, yet a young man who was out to enjoy all the pleasures of youth. But life had changed for me just four weeks previously. Now I was listening to the sailor in his efforts to preach.

He was most certainly a keen Christian, very zealous, not exactly tactful; his speech was ungrammatical, and his message quite spontaneous, totally unprepared. He just talked. Suddenly he realised that perhaps he had talked enough! He turned to me and said, 'Over to you, brother. Just you carry on.' I had never preached in my life, was totally unprepared, and everyone knew me in that village. One month before I had been shocked into reality by hearing a message on the Lord's second coming, had gone back to my digs, knelt by my bed, and thanked the Lord Jesus for dying for me.

The sailor continued, 'Don't be afraid, brother. Open

your mouth wide and he will fill it.' I wondered just what he meant, but thought that I could at least try and tell of my recent experience of conversion. I knew that I had been born anew, but I had had no training, and there was no time now to prepare! In rather faltering terms I started to tell what Jesus Christ meant to me now. To make things ten times worse, I turned my head slightly and saw my Aunt and Uncle coming along the street. Uncle was headmaster of a big school in the Medway towns. Auntie looked the other way (I don't blame her), and Uncle nodded curtly. What I said at that open air meeting I do not know, and I am sure that no one else ever remembered. After about five minutes I shut up, shook hands with the sailor, jumped on my cycle and went to tell my Christian friends at the farm of my escapade. My pulses were racing, my heart leaped for joy, but I there and then resolved that I would never again go into action without a carefully prepared message.

Three months later a missionary from Algeria visited our church. He told of a visit that he had recently made to a part of Algeria that was completely unevangelised. In one village, the Muslim men had pleaded with him to settle among them, promising to give him a one-roomed house rent-free, five fig trees, a salary of about five pounds per year, a sheep at their annual feast, and as many eggs as he could eat. 'The door is wide open to reach this tribe, the people are without a witness for Christ, and there is no one to go,' he said. 'The Lord Jesus said, ''Go into all the world and preach the gospel to every creature,'' and that includes Muslims.' I listened to him as he told of this open door, and felt an inner urge, the prompting of the Holy Spirit, convincing me that I must go to Algeria. God had a work for me to do there. This was God's work, but it was also to be *my* work. We sang the hymn, 'Thy life was given for me: What have I given for thee?' and it was during the singing of that hymn that I decided to place my life completely under the control of the Lord Jesus. With all my heart I sang that last verse, 'To thee my all I bring, my Saviour and my *King*.'

My whole life had to be replanned. The training at the Agricultural College was abandoned. I remained on the farm for three long years. I started to study my Bible each evening, learned New Testament Greek, and planned systematic study of the New Testament. I went round the villages of Kent preaching each Saturday afternoon during the summer months, and took a boys' Bible class. Soon after that I met Pearl Lamb who had been born in Algeria, and I was sure that she was the most charming girl in the world, a conviction that has grown through the years.

I was not the only boy who felt that way but we became engaged, an engagement which was to last for five long years. Pearl trained as a nurse at the Mildmay Memorial Hospital, with a princely salary of one pound a month. As she was born in Algeria she had no church to sponsor her, but somehow she managed to save enough to provide her meagre outfit. There followed those long years of waiting when our spirits chafed at the discipline of marking time, but had it not been for those years of testing in the homeland we would never have been able to face the long years of arduous service that followed. One thing we knew. We had been called. We must go forward.

I spent one year in training at Livingstone College, where I had training in Medicine and Surgery and allied subjects; and then went to All Nations Bible College. In the final exams at both Colleges I managed to take first place.

In October 1925 we travelled through France to Marseilles, and from that port crossed to Algiers by boat. I spent three months brushing up my schoolboy French, and then tackled the difficult Berber language, Kabyle. Pearl already knew the two languages, and needed simply to learn to read Kabyle and to study

Kabyle grammar. We were married in Algiers in the month of May 1927. In order to commence the Lord's work as soon as possible, and to avoid undue expense, we decided to forego a honeymoon; we spent just one day at a seaside resort. Then we took the long train journey to Setif, where we spent the night. A week previously I had visited Setif with a senior missionary, in obedience to the decision of the Mission that the large Arabic-speaking town should serve as a base from which we would operate. I had worked hard to acquire a good knowledge of Kabyle, but it was never spoken at Setif. The nearest Kabyle village was fifty miles away. With a heavy heart I had tramped the streets of that town looking for a small apartment that we could rent. We found nothing. It was then that my senior missionary suggested that we might travel to the Guergour tribes of Kabylia before we gave up the search.

We stood on the narrow stony track nearly five thousand feet high in the mountains of Lesser Kabylia. Nearly fifty miles away, the snow-capped Atlas mountains raised their heads. Range after range of mountains and foothills extended as far as the eye could see; the villages fringing the hill tops. I gazed entranced at the magnificent panorama. At our feet was a group of villages, each with its mosque into which the men streamed for the Friday noon prayer. The low monotonous chanting of the boys and students arose as they recited the Koran; and the strident voice of the muezzin rang out calling the faithful to prayer. More than fifty villages were visible, and hundreds more lay hidden in the valleys and behind the mountains.

'These people have never heard of our Saviour,' said my companion. 'No one has ever told them the wonderful news of salvation.' Deep in my heart the conviction was born, 'I am the man to tell them. This is my corner of the great world field.' A deep compassion, an irresistible yearning, gripped my soul. During the forty years of service that followed I could never look out over that vast panorama of mountains without being deeply moved, and feeling the continual yearning to reach out to those villages to tell of new life through Christ.

'We must be getting back,' said my companion, 'but on our way we will call at the administrative centre of Lafayette, and see if we can find a house for you to live in. I must warn you that this is extremely unlikely, and the Mission said that you must work in the town of Setif.' (Ten minutes after arriving at Lafayette the house was found, and secured by the payment of the first month's rent. There was no long search. Thus God confirmed his call to us, through the workings of his providence, and the inward urge of the Holy Spirit.)

At five o'clock the next morning we found our way to the bus station, and left on a ramshackle bus for Lafayette. People looked at us with undisguised interest. Neither Europeans nor Arabs had ever seen missionaries before. How strangely alone and inexperienced we felt. The bleak barren mountains of the High Plateaux were in striking contrast to the beautiful country of Kabylia. We soon discovered that, although Lafayette was the administrative centre of the Kabyle tribes of the Guergour, the language of the people was Arabic. The first Kabyle villages were still twenty miles distant, and we had no means of transport. Our aim was to evangelise the Kabyles, we knew their language, but how could we reach them? They are said to be the descendants of the Amorites of the Old Testament. When the Arabs invaded Algeria in AD 647 they drove the Kabyles into the mountains. They destroyed the Christian churches and the Berbers became Muslims. Their religion is Islam; the word means 'surrender to God.' A man who follows Islam is called a Muslim, or Moslem; which means he professes to surrender himself wholly to the will of Allah. He believes in Allah who is unique, all-powerful and merciful; in his angels and spirits; in the four great revealed books: the Law of Moses, the Psalms of David, the Gospel of Jesus and the Koran of Mohammed. They also believe in 124,000 prophets and apostles that Allah has sent, in the day of resurrection and in heaven and hell. A good Muslim is always prepared to repeat the *shahada* and say, 'I witness that there is no God but Allah, and that Mohammed is the Messenger of Allah.' He is supposed to pray five times a day, to pay the ritual alms, to abstain from eating and drinking during the month of Ramadhan, and if he can afford it, to make the pilgrimage to the Kaaba in Mecca at least once in his lifetime.

The Kabyles are a white-skinned race with European characteristics. Their mountain strongholds were never fully subdued by the successive invasions of Romans, Arabs, Turks and French. They have retained their own language, which missionaries and others have reduced to writing. The language varies from tribe to tribe and often from village to village. Many of the Kabyles are highly intelligent, and can compete with Europeans in every sphere of university and business life. They are capable of intense and strong emotions, are deeply affectionate to their friends, but bitterly opposed to their enemies, and can become bigoted religious fanatics. A Kabyle is trustworthy and will never betray a friend, or one who is under his protection; and for this characteristic I owe them a debt of deep gratitude that I can never repay. The people can be divided into two classes, Kabyles and Marabouts, but all speak Kabyle and all are ardent Muslims. The Marabouts are the upper class and claim to be the direct racial descendants of Mohammed. They are men and women of character; and even though they may be desperately poor they are genteel and polite. These are the people to whom God sent us.

Chapter Two

Facing the Challenge

Each day a bus left Lafayette between noon and three o'clock for Kabylia, returning the next morning. We were able to rent an unfurnished room in the courtyard of a Kabyle house at Guenzet, and it was here that we planned to spend two nights each week. The seats of the bus were made to accommodate five persons, but frequently eight were crammed into this limited space. The thick woollen burnouses worn by the men restricted any movement once people were packed in like sardines. The roof was loaded with merchandise of every description, including live sheep and chickens. When no more people could be packed into the limited interior of the vehicle, others were told to climb on the roof. There they sat with their feet over the sides dangling in the faces of the passengers below! In places the road was so narrow that it was impossible for the bus to negotiate the corners. It would proceed as far as possible, reverse, and then just manage to scrape the cliff face on one side with the motor overhanging the precipice! There were many exciting and hair-raising episodes.

There were numerous accidents on these dangerous mountainous roads. We will never forget the truck which got out of control, overturned and caught fire. Within seconds it was a blazing inferno. Ten veiled women had been packed into the back part, together with two sheep and several children. The canvas back and sides had been tightly laced so that no one could see the women. They could not get out, and the two men in front made no attempt to save them. They were all burned to death. *'Mektoub*—It was decreed, what could we do?' was the explanation given to the investigating police. That is Islam.

God in his mercy protected us throughout the years from any serious accident. On this, our first trip on one of these decrepit buses, we arrived in the large village of Guenzet just before dark. A motley crowd of men and children met the bus, and there was much speculation as to our identity. We were glad to gain the shelter of our rented room. It measured nine feet square, with a stone cobbled floor, and a thatched roof from which dropped a succession of small insects. There was no window, no fireplace, no light. The floor was reeking with moisture, and it had been used to store salt. We were to spend two nights each week in this cold, damp, unfurnished room.

Having unpacked our bags and eaten our cold supper by the light of a candle, we prepared to sleep on the one camp bed that we possessed. It would not accommodate us both, so in spite of the state of the floor, we spread the sleeping bag on a ground sheet. The moisture soon seeped through both ground sheet and bag. There was little sleep that night.

At 4 a.m. the call of the muezzin rang out over the sleeping village where we had spent the night. It was taken up by each of the eight mosques. 'Come to prayer. Prayer is better than sleep.' How near to us it seemed. The challenge came to us from every side. The low drone of voices came over as the men recited their prayers. Now it was time for me to go to the mosque and make the acquaintance of these fanatical men; to win them from antagonism to allegiance to the King of Kings. How weak we felt! We bowed our heads in prayer.

'We rest on thee'—our Shield and our Defender!
We go not forth alone against the foe;
  Strong in thy strength, safe in thy keeping tender,
'We rest on thee, and in thy name we go.'

The sun was just rising above the horizon as I left the shelter of that room. 'The Lord be with you, darling, I shall be praying for you,' said Pearl. She turned the key in the lock, shutting herself in to commence her lonely vigil. Never before had I felt my utter weakness. My heart was filled with misgivings and fears. 'I rest on thee, and in thy name I go.' I reached the mosque. The men had finished their prayer and were sitting on the stone benches. Others were standing round discussing plans for the day. I sat down.

'*Sebah kum belkheyr* (Good morning to you all)', I said.

'*Merahba bik* (Welcome),' they replied. 'Tell us, are you a good Muslim? Have you prayed the morning prayer?'

'Witness to Mohammed. Say there is no god but God . . .'

'Was Jesus the Son of God? Or was he just the son of Mary?'

'Tell us, how many prophets are there?'

'Who is the last, the greatest, the seal of the prophets?'

'Did Jesus die, or was he taken alive to heaven?'

The questions came in rapid succession, and to attempt to answer them was useless. They did not mean that I should.

I produced my New Testament in Kabyle and read a verse or two.

'We do not understand that book. It is not our language. It is not even good Kabyle,' they said.

They did not want to listen. Their voices increased to a loud roar, while Pearl listened from the shelter of that windowless room. She wondered if I should be torn to pieces by that fanatical mob.

She dared not come and join me, but she could pray. How thankful she was at the end of an hour to hear my knock, and to see my face once again, still smiling after the bitter words. We joined in a cup of coffee before setting out to tramp to the surrounding villages.

A discreet cough outside told us that someone had called. It was the young Kabyle man who had rented the room to us. He was immaculately dressed in a European suit, but wore a white turban and black patent shoes. He was obviously a Kabyle gentleman who knew how to behave. He accepted a cup of coffee, and my wife produced the cake which she had made at home, and which was to last us for three days. Cutting a slice of the cake, she offered it to our visitor. 'Thank you so much,' he replied, 'but it is rather a lot.' Then, to her consternation, he took the cake, leaving the slice! This was true etiquette, for the host always breaks off a piece of the bread, and eats it to show that the food is not poisoned. Then he hands the remainder to his guest. True politeness, but she knew better next time. That is how one learns!

As soon as our visitor had left, we set out to walk to the villages. The surrounding landscape was pictur-esque and delightfully green in the morning sun. Behind us the mountains were covered with a forest of cork oak and aleppo pine. To our left, in the distance, a series of bare scree-girt ridges were scoured by deep gorges and ravines. The swift flowing streams of the winter were beginning to dry up. The slopes of the mountain below us were terraced to provide small gardens where vines, pomegranates and figs would flourish later in the year. The fields on the lower slopes were divided into minute plots, where barley, lentils, peas and beans were growing. Prickly pears grew everywhere and there were a few isolated orange trees. We were struck by the resemblance to the biblical description of Canaan in Deuteronomy 8:7-9.

At the entrance to the first village, custom decreed that we must separate, I to go to the men in the mosque, and Pearl to the women in their houses. The heavy oak doors of every house were shut and barred from within. How could Pearl, a young English bride, contact those frightened isolated women, shut away as they were in their harems? She had been brought up in a Kabyle village, and knew well the women's abject fear of strangers, their unwillingness to open the door to anyone whom they did not know. Yet she longed to make contact with them, to be friendly, to sit with them on their mats and talk. A sudden thought struck her. Thirsty and weary as she was with her long walk, she could ask for a drink of water. Knocking gently on one door she called,

'*A thamrarth*—old woman, open the door.' The door was opened a fraction of an inch and the frightened face of a young woman peered out.

'Go away quickly. Clear out. We do not want you,' she said.

'*Sebah alkheyr*—Good morning,' was the friendly greeting.

'Oh, so you are a Kabyle,' said the woman. Her fears were dispelled. This stranger could speak her language, and she spoke it well.

'Who are you? What do you want? Please, oh please go away.'

'I am so thirsty. Please give me a drink.'

'Yes, we have a well in our courtyard. Come in and sit down.'

Pearl went into the courtyard, a rush mat was brought and she sat down. In a few moments she was surrounded by all the women of the house, who touched her hair, stroked her dress, and lifted it up to see what she wore underneath! The bucket was lowered into the well with the long cord of plaited goat's hair, and the pitcher was filled with fresh cold water. Pearl shuddered. She knew that such water might be contaminated, but there was nothing for it. She had asked for a drink, and now she must drink the water. She tilted the pitcher in such a way that the water ran into her open mouth without touching the vessel with her lips.

'*Alhamdouallah* (Praise the Lord),' she said when she had drunk. '*Sahha* (health)!' came from every woman.

'Thank you. May he give you all good health,' she replied.

Then she produced her New Testament in Kabyle, and read to them the story of Jesus and the woman at the well. How surprised they were that a woman could read! Never, never in their lives had they heard of such a thing. Only boys and men learned to read. She read on: 'Everyone who drinks this water will be thirsty again, but whoever drinks the water I give him will never thirst. Indeed, the water I give him will become in him a spring of water welling up to eternal life.' The women listened intently, gripped by the message.

Suddenly their faces changed colour, fear and terror seized them. Turning round, Pearl understood the reason. Coming towards her was an old hag with a demonic expression on her face. She seemed the very personification of evil. She was the old lady of the house, and ruled her household with a rod of iron. She had suffered in her youth and was determined to make her daughters-in-law suffer by every means in her power. Now one of them had dared to let this stranger into their courtyard, into her house. She would pay dearly for this, but first the stranger must be dealt with. Meanwhile every woman fled.

'What has brought you here? You have come here to tell these stories about your Jesus. May God curse you and your religion,' she howled. Nearer and nearer she drew, until her evil face almost touched the pure face of the girl. Her vile breath was sickening.

'Come into this room and talk,' she said. Pearl went in, and the old hag slammed the door, and turned the key in the lock.

'Now I have got you,' she said, 'I will shut you up and force you to marry my son. You will just disappear. Before your husband knows where you are it will be too late. I'll teach you. Take that, and that!' She spat again and again; her spittle directed full into Pearl's face. Again she spat and cursed, working herself into a frenzy of rage.

Suddenly the old woman opened the door of the courtyard, and with a tremendous effort, thrust the servant of God outside. She fell headlong in the dust and dirt of the narrow lane. She had come to win these women for Christ, come with a message of love, only to be met with bitter hatred and scorn.

She rose from the ground, the dust and filth clinging to that awful spittle. Women appeared from nowhere. They pulled her into a neighbouring courtyard, wiped the filth from her dress, and offered clean water for her to wash her face and hands.

'Come into our yard,' they said, 'That old woman is cruel and wicked. Her daughters-in-law have told us of your wonderful Book. Please read it to us.'

'But how did you get here when you are shut away?' asked Pearl.

'Oh, that is easy. We climbed over the roof and dropped down into the yard from that fig tree. Look, here come some more now.'

Three more women had climbed into the fig tree from the roof, and now dropped to the ground in the courtyard.

'We are waiting for a new bride to be brought,' they said. 'Read something to us while we are waiting.'

So the Lord began to open doors.

On that first day we visited four villages before returning to our room. We usually found the Kabyles very hospitable; and they welcomed us to their village; but as soon as they found out the object of our visit their attitude would change to hostility and suspicion. The bus left at five o'clock on the following morning for the return journey, but we had to be at the terminus at least half-an-hour beforehand, in order to get a place. It was with a certain sense of satisfaction that we reached home at Lafayette for breakfast at seven o'clock.

A week later an experienced missionary accompanied me on a visit to Guenzet while Pearl remained at home. Together we sat on the large stone slabs in front of the mosque of that fanatical village. Nearly a hundred men had gathered, and my colleague, who spoke Kabyle well, spoke to them from the Psalms. 'Blessed is he whose transgressions are forgiven, whose sins are covered.'

'There is no forgiveness for anyone outside the religion of Islam,' shouted the sheikh, the religious leader of the village.

'Do you believe in Mohammed?' said another.

'We do not want to hear about Moses and David and Jesus, but only about Mohammed,' yelled a third, with a scornful smirk on his face.

'*Chehed* (witness), and say, "There is no god but Allah, and Mohammed is the Apostle of God!" '

In a moment every man was on his feet, shouting vociferously.

'Testify, testify to Mohammed. Tell us that you believe in him. May God curse your religion! May he blind you! May he send you to hell fire! May he give you a jackal to bite you!'

Malicious curses were hurled at us from every quarter. A hand shot out and struck my throat. The unexpected blow caused me to stagger backwards. Another man deliberately cleared his throat and spat viciously. The tumult was such that my colleague could proceed no further in spite of his long experience. He had read just one verse of a Psalm, and now with the awful din, it was impossible for him to be heard. The situation was extremely ugly. How could we escape from this angry mob? In fanatical frenzy the Muslims shouted and screamed, moving closer and closer. The old missionary folded his arms, gazed at them, and smiled. If he was perturbed, he did not show it.

'Look, he is not afraid. He is laughing at us,' they said. There was a moment of dead silence, the tension lessened.

'Come along, we must go,' he said, and the crowd opened to let us pass.

'Go, and may the curse of God rest on you for ever.' The voice of the old Muslim sheikh rang out in a final malediction. He had succeeded in driving us from his village.

Once away from the village, the veteran missionary turned to me and said, 'You must never, no *never*, return here alone. It is far too dangerous. You will be killed.'—But God had called me. God had sent me to those villages, to these tribes of fanatical men. I *must* go back—alone.

So, from the very first days we realised that we were engaged in a spiritual conflict. We had come with a message of good will, only to be met with bitter antagonism and intense hatred. We could say with Paul,

Our fight is not against any physical enemy: it is against organisations and powers that are spiritual. We are up against the unseen power that controls this dark world, and the spiritual agents from the very headquarters of evil. (*Ephesians 6:10, Phillips.*)

Could we possibly win through in the face of this bitter opposition? I alone with the men? Pearl alone with the women? The Lord sent out his disciples two by two, but because we were workers among Muslims we had to plough a lone furrow. Workers are so few. In those early days of our missionary life, Pearl sometimes accompanied me to the villages; but a strange man can never enter a Muslim house with his wife. She could never sit with me among the men. Each of us must go alone. Two lone workers among a population of over a quarter of a million. Could we possibly succeed? Could we win at least some of these people for our Lord? Throughout that first summer and autumn we continued these weekly visits, but the method was terribly time consuming. How we needed a motor cycle and sidecar! The Lord knew, and without any seeking on our part, he provided a small car.

Chapter Three

Outreach

The provision of a small car enabled us to extend the range of activities greatly. We eventually evangelised over five hundred villages in our area. These villages are often perched on the mounatain crests, and sometimes hidden in the valleys. In places there are as many as six hundred inhabitants to the square mile. Each village is administered by an assembly of elders, and the chief of these is called the *amin*. Local codes of law deal with all questions of property and general offences.

Each village can be traced back to the man who in antiquity was its founder. His sons married and formed the various quarters of the village. Villages are usually divided into *sofs*, or rival clans, which were originally matrimonial fractions.

Of the five hundred villages which I visited more or less regularly with the gospel, only twenty-five were situated on any sort of motor road. The rest had to be reached on foot. This meant tramping for four to six hours a day over rough stony roads, fording streams, climbing up to a village four thousand feet up and then down to the valley, before climbing up to the next village. My wife could not acompany me to these places, I had no fellow worker, so I went alone.

Some places could be reached in a day. I would then drive out in the car, leave it on the roadside, and in the early morning, often before it was light, slip away for the long walk. At night I would return to the car to find it intact, untouched and ready for the journey home. On only one occasion during thirty seven years was it broken into, and then by a stranger to the district. Another set of villages could be reached by spending the night in a distant village, visiting hamlets and villages on the way out and back. This would occupy two days. A third group could only be reached by an extended effort. Loading all that I needed for ten days or more on to the back of a donkey, I would tramp from village to village. Alternatively, I would take a tent and pitch it at convenient points along the motor road, walking down to the villages during the day and return- ing to the tent each night. Every spring and autumn, for a period of ten days, I used to make a special effort to reach these distant tribes.

The Kabyles are a community-loving people and when the day's work is ended, they gather in groups in the mosque, the local coffee house, or the local *thejmath*. The *thejmath* is a covered building at the entrance to the village. It is here that the village elders meet. It is bordered by large flat stones which serve as seats, worn smooth and shiny by years of use. The Kabyles are most industrious and during the day they work in the fields, ploughing, sowing, reaping, gather- ing olives or figs, or making olive oil with their primi- tive olive presses that date from biblical times. In the summer, during the heat of the day, twenty or thirty men will gather in the *thejmath*, and towards sunset as many as a hundred. This is the best place for an open air meeting, and a respectful hearing is usually given to the message.

It was four o'clock in the morning on a cold winter's day. Hoar frost covered the ground, there was the nip of snow in the air, and the supper slopes of the surroun- ding mountains were already deep in snow. Bed was certainly the best place on such a day! Yet there were still hundreds of people in those villages who had never heard the good news. So, out of the warm bed, a quick cup of coffee, a bite of bread and a rapid check up. The previous evening I had packed into my bag some tracts, a Bible, sandwiches for midday, an orange, a handful of figs, dental forceps, a mac and (last but not least) a good selection of literature supplied by the Scripture Gift Mission in French, Kabyle and Arabic. Locking the front door of home behind me, I went out into the night.

The morning star shone brightly in the east; the smallest sound echoed in the clear mountain air as I drove along the winding road, the frost crackling under the wheels. A sudden turn in the road, and dark forms loomed up in the car lights. I stepped on the brakes only just in time to avoid a herd of twenty camels lumbering along with their clumsy gait, each carrying a quarter of a ton of wheat. Half an hour later I reached a suitable spot for parking the car, just off the road. The first streaks of dawn were visible in the east. Not a soul could be seen as I locked the car door, and committed it to the keeping of the One who through the years had never failed. I went down to the river, took off my boots and socks, rolled my trousers as high as possible and stepped into the icy water. It swirled by swiftly, swollen by the melting snow. It was bitterly cold. In spite of myself tears filled my eyes. Large stones, rolled along by the torrent, battered my ankles and legs. I forged on even though at times I nearly lost my footing. Suddenly I stumbled into a hole in midstream, and plunged into water up to my hips. 'What a fool you are; go back,' said an inner voice. 'Go on,' said my Lord. I knew that I was a man under orders, and I must go on. Hurling my boots across the river, I pushed on step by step. There could be no going back then. Wet and cold, my clothes soaked with icy water, I reached the further bank. Wringing the water from my sodden clothes, I put on my socks and boots, and set off on that long six-mile walk to the first village.

The sun rose above the hills as I toiled up the last long climb to the village, gasping for breath with the effort. The men were sitting round the small square and I greeted them:

'Good morning to you all,' I said. 'May God give you a good morning,' they replied.

'Where have you come from?'   'Where did you spend the night?'

'In my own home,' I answered.

'Impossible.'

'Well, I did.'

'Then who carried you over the river? You have no animal.'

'I forded the river as you do. I just came through on my feet.'

'But why so early in the morning?'

'I think you all know why. I have a message for you from the Word of God. Will you stay and listen?' They did.

The men quickly brought a large mat which they spread on the ground so that I could sit down. Taking off my boots, I sat cross-legged on the mat, and waited for the men to gather round. Some still stood at a distance, but when I produced a large picture of the Brazen Serpent, they too came over. I spread the picture on the mat, opened my Bible and gave them time to examine the painting, ask questions and comment. Then when a sizeable group had gathered, I read to them John 3:14-20. The meeting lasted nearly an hour, for I had to answer their questions and apply the message to their own lives. The meeting over, one man said, 'Come along to my house and share my breakfast. At this time of year we eat before we go to work in the fields.' We went into a closed-in yard and the man called to his wife, 'Smail, bring the mat.' A man will never call his wife by name or speak of her. He uses the name of his eldest son to call her. The woman came out carrying the mat, but turning her face away from us so that I should not see her. Shortly afterwards she return with a basket on which was a hot loaf of bread and some figs. The bread had been made into cakes about fifteen inches in diameter and half an inch thick. She had baked them on a griddle over the wood fire. The art of cooking is to turn the bread at the appropriate moment, so that both sides are equally cooked. This was cooked to perfection. The man broke the bread into pieces, ate a piece himself and handed me the rest. Breaking off a small piece, I dipped it into the bowl of olive oil and munched it with a fig. It was a wholesome breakfast to which I did justice after my long walk. Again the woman called her husband, who went away and returned bringing a dish of olive oil in which floated four raw eggs. He said, 'You need strength to walk over our mountains.' I said the missionaries' prayer, 'Lord, I'll get it down, you please keep it down,' and managed to swallow two of the eggs.

Then he took me to see a poor suffering lad who had not left the dark room in which he lay for many months. He was a bag of bones, covered with bed sores, and the stench was abominable. No doctor ever visited this village, so I cared for the lad as best I could, and left a note for someone to bring to the dispensary for further dressings. Then I started to walk to the next village.

I soon discovered that sharing in some measure their lives, facing their hardships, eating their food, caring for their sick, sitting where they sat, listening, sympathising, was the way to Kabyle hearts. This was the Lord's way. This was Paul's way. So it was that over the years I saw the attitude of these rough mountaineers gradually change from hostility to friendliness and trust.

When I left the village, the men were already setting out to work. Driving a couple of oxen before them, carrying the heavy plough on their shoulders, they walked from two to five miles each day to their fields. The next village was three miles away, and there I found a smaller group surrounding blind Hamid. He was expounding to them the doctrines of the Koran, emphasising his words with a stick which he held out before him. Afflicted by blindness from his birth, unable to work, he had spent many years in a Koranic school, listening to others repeating the lines of their sacred book, until he too had learned to recite it by heart.

He knew all the favourite arguments of the local sheikhs, and the basic doctrines of Islam. I sat down with the men. The blind man stopped, and for a few minutes listened attentively to the gospel message. Then he opened fire with a volley of questions. He did not wait for me to reply to any of them. He did not want an answer. His aim was to show how much he, a blind man, knew about his religion. At any price he must stop these other men from hearing the message of life that I had brought. I did my best to reply to his questions, to show sympathy and love, but he became more and more excited, and the meeting was degenerating into a useless discussion. I decided that I would try a method which had often succeeded.

'Tell us what Mohammed has really done for you, my friend. I will give you ten minutes to tell us, and during that time I will remain silent. Then you will listen for ten minutes as I tell you what Christ has done for me.' The bargain was struck.

'You speak first, Hamid.'

He began, 'Mohammed has told us to bear witness to him, to pray five times a day, to fast, to give alms, to read the Koran. That is what he has done for us Muslims.'

'Go on, tell us what he has *done* for you,' I pleaded.

A full minute passed, but Hamid needed no more time. Mohammed had told him to do so much. He knew it all by heart, but . . . Then very simply, from a heart full of love for my Saviour and for these men, I told then of all that he had done for me. 'The Lord Jesus has saved me. He has transformed my life. He is my constant friend and companion. He has given me a life of fulfilment and joy. He gives me the strength to follow the commandments of God, and the assurance of forgiveness when I fail. He has taught me to love my enemies. He is soon coming back to earth, not to reign for forty years, but to reign for ever. He is coming to take me to be with him.' Poor blind Hamid could contain himself no longer. He cursed me and spat at me, adding insult to insult. It was useless to continue. I left.

Walking down the village street I could still see the upturned face, the gesticulating stick, the vehement way in which Hamid cursed and spat in my direction. Oh, the infinite pathos of those sightless eyes, as that ignorant Muslim tried to teach his fellow Muslims, a blind leader of the blind. I made my way to the next village, reflecting on the seeming paradox that this bitter opposition in one village is often counteracted by deep heart hunger in the next. Yet how true to the pattern in the Acts of the Apostles.

An hour's walk brought me to the first houses of the next village. Piles of black olives were spread out in the sun. A middle-aged man was buying them, weighing them on a large weighing-machine.

'Where are you going, sheikh?' he said.

'I am going to the coffee house to speak to the men about God.'

'Well, just sit down and tell me here.'

'No, I am going where I can find the men, and they will be free to listen.'

'OK then, I will come too, for last week my son was in your meeting, and he told us all that he had heard. We do believe in Jesus, but we do not understand his work. We want to know.' He left his work to come and listen.

The coffee house was crowded with men. Some were playing dominoes, some gambling with cards, some merely sipping cups of black coffee. I removed my shoes at the door, and left them with those of the other men, then walked across the mats and sat down. I ordered a cup of coffee and watched it being prepared. A small charcoal fire was burning in the angle made by the two walls. Over this fire a tin of water was continually boiling. The proprietor put several spoonfuls of coffee powder into a small coffee pot, and added as many spoonfuls of sugar. The coffee beans had been pounded to a fine powder with a pestle made from the axle of a lorry, in a mortar hewed from solid stone by the Romans centuries before! The coffee pot was a small tin soldered on to a short handle about one foot long. Each customer's coffee was freshly prepared in a separate pot; and seven or eight of these were standing round the charcoal fire. The coffee was brought to the boil, and as it rose in the pot it was tapped lightly. The hot coffee in the pot subsided and was boiled again. This was done three times. The extreme cold season had passed, or the man would have added cayenne pepper to give an added zest. The proprietor poured the thick syrupy mixture into a small tin pot with a tiny lid, placed it beside a cup, and handed it to me on a brass plate. I sipped it for a few minutes, meanwhile making as much noise as possible in order to show my appreciation of their excellent coffee. Then I appealed to the men to leave their games for just ten minutes while I read to them from the Book. I had to condense the message, so read 1 Timothy 1:15, and told them of the purpose of Christ's coming into the world. I was most impressed by the attitude of one man who listened intently. There was a moment's distraction outside. In a minute the coffee shop emptied. The interested man remained. Drawing near to me he whispered,

'Tell me just what I am to believe.'

I read to him from Isaiah 53:6. 'The Lord has laid on him the iniquity of us all.'

'Ah, I see now, my sins on him. He carried them. He

paid, so I am free. Thank you.'

The men returned, and once more he was a Muslim among Muslims. I finished the message and prepared to leave. Once more the man spoke up,

'Tell me, sheikh, are there any who believe in the Lord Jesus in this land? Any Kabyles?'

Oh, the dread of being alone, the only Christian among hostile Muslims.

Another half-an-hour's walk brought me to the next village. I at once went to the small mosque in the centre of the village. It was there that the men usually congregated, sitting on the flag stones which paved the yard in front of it. No men were to be seen, but the drone of voices came from the interior. A lad informed me that a new Muslim sheikh had been installed, and that he had insisted that the entire male population came daily to the mosque to learn the Koran. It was so obvious that I was unwanted, and I did not wish to intrude; so rather sadly, I shouldered my bag and walked away. I had not gone more than ten paces when a man called to me from the mosque,

'O sheikh, surely you are not going away without reading to us? Have you no message at all for us from the Word of God?'

'But you have engaged a new sheikh who is teaching you the Koran, and you certainly do not want me now.'

'Come back to us. Come into the mosque and read to us,' was the reply.

The invitation was too good to be refused. I removed my boots at the entrance to the mosque, placed them with those of the men, and went in to be introduced to the new sheikh. To my astonishment the men said to him, 'Put away your books, this man came and taught us when we had no one to help us. We are going to listen to what he says.'

Then they turned to me and said,

'We are waiting, sheikh. Read to us.'

The new Koranic sheikh listened for about ten minutes, and then rose and left without a word. The other men all remained for half-an-hour, and seemed to greatly appreciate the talk.

I visited just one other village before setting out on the long walk back to the car. Fording the river I found the car just as I had left it. God had watched over it. I soon covered the half-hour's run home. I had been away just fourteen hours. A normal day's work.

Chapter Four

Taking the Offensive

We never intended that Lafayette should be a mission station, but rather a centre from which we could radiate to the surrounding tribes. At the same time, we realised that there was a tremendous spiritual need right on our doorstep, both among Muslims and Europeans. We soon started classes for Muslim boys and girls. These classes were held in our living room, and by the end of the class, the furniture was often thick with mud. Every Sunday fifteen to twenty French people attended a service in our home. We had only three rooms and a kitchen, plus a toilet in a public yard, to reach which involved a walk of one hundred yards up the street! Such minor inconveniences are to be expected when you are pioneer missionaries. It was delightful to be able to use our home for the Lord, the living room serving as dining room, class room, meeting room for gospel services, dental clinic, and reception room for visitors.

God worked among the Roman Catholics in those early days and the landlord's wife professed conversion. He was very annoyed, and in order to prevent us having any further influence on her, he sold the house over our heads, and we received notice to quit. It was impossible to find even one room to make our home. God's work was going ahead so well. We had succeeded in making contact with so many Muslims; scores of children were attending the classes. Many homes were open. Contacts had been made among the men. God was working. Then the blow fell—notice to quit. We were homeless, put on the street, with no right of appeal. In fellowship with our Lord, we had nowhere to lay our heads. The French judge was exceedingly kind, and found us a house in an Arab village, six miles away; but we did not know Arabic, only French and Kabyle. With heavy hearts we loaded our few belongings on to a lorry, and set off for this village where we would be the only Europeans. It was also the most fanatical Muslim village of the whole area. How depressed and downcast we felt, as we said 'Goodbye' to our first home.

The place to which God in his infinite wisdom took us was called Hammam. Although its inhabitants were almost exclusively Arab, a few Kabyle women were married to Arab men. Pearl was able to contact these through her excellent knowledge of their language. I had to tackle my fourth language in three years. I started a dispensary, held classes for boys, and meetings for men. Soon crowds of people were coming for treatment. As my knowledge of their language increased, so did numbers. The Lord's blessing rested on the work even in those early days. Souls were saved. For thirty five years the Lord's work was continued in that fanatical centre. As many as 8,000 patients were treated each year, and the gospel message was spread over a wide area. The Lord sent us to this strategic centre, and to do so he used what Satan intended as a knock-out blow. Satan is strong, but God is Sovereign. He is all-wise and Almighty. He makes all things to work together for good to those who love him. But the successive blows are sometimes hard to bear.

The village of Hammam proved to be a most interesting place. Extensive Roman ruins were a continual reminder that in the early centuries of the Christian era, this place had been the seat of two bishoprics, Roman and Donatist. A stone bearing the names of twelve men who had been martyred for their Christian faith reminded us that many early Christians, who had been faithful to their Lord, had suffered in this very village. In the mountains above there were extensive underground passages and catacombs, telling of those who were driven underground because they loved the Lord. How these corridors must have echoed with the hymns and praises of those who sang the songs of Zion. The hot radioactive waters of the Hammam had been exploited by the Romans centuries before. They had constructed extensive and elaborate public baths (Hammam means 'Bath'), the remains of which could be clearly seen, and some of which were still in use. For most of the year, and especially during the spring and summer months, large crowds of sick people flocked for healing to this thermal centre, many of them coming long distances. It was very evident that this was a strategic centre, and it was up to us to exploit the situation.

The population of the surrounding areas also discovered that I had some knowledge of medicine. There was only one French doctor for a population of over 100,000 people. He lived several miles away, and because I travelled about in the villages, he graciously consented to allow the work at Hammam to go on. It was quickly evident that by caring for the sick, and seeking to alleviate suffering, we could not only render service to people, but give them some tangible evidence of our concern for them. The entire population of the Hammam was Muslim, most of them being of the Marabout, or priestly, caste. Everyone knew that they were religious fanatics who would persistently oppose and persecute any who became Christian. But the Lord Jesus had said: 'Love your enemies, do good to those who hate you.' He himself had exercised a healing ministry. He was moved with compassion by the sight of crowds of sick and suffering people, and he healed them all. When he sent out his disciples, he gave them power to heal every sort of sickness and disease. Practical love is a most effective weapon in spiritual warfare.

We were continually extending our outreach to homes and villages, but it was much more difficult to induce the people to come to us, and to gather in a place where they could quietly listen to the message. How could we persuade men to come? The answer was the small clinic where those who were sick could find relief and healing, and which the timid and reticent could use an excuse for attending. We had neither the training or the resources to open a hospital, but in the dispensary we were able to devote more time and energy to the spiritual side of the work. So we announced that twice weekly we would see sick people in the garage adjoining our home.

As I moved about among the people I was horrified to see the suffering brought about through ignorance, neglect and the absence of a skilled practitioner. The people had their own crude methods of caring for the sick and injured, but all too often they only aggravated the pain and suffering. In one isolated village I found a boy with a compound fracture of the radius. This had been 'set' by a Kabyle bone-setter. Four small pieces of wood six inches long and one inch wide had been bound tightly round the injured arm. The hand and the arm above the wound had swollen to twice their normal size, and the tissues immediately surrounding the wound had shrunk. The ends of the bone had pierced the skin and were rubbing against the splints. The whole was a suppurating mass which had been covered with a black sticky preparation resembling tar. The stench was unbearable, and the poor lad had been in this state for nearly a month.

How ignorant are some of the poor women! A baby boy was afflicted with measles. As is so often the case, eye trouble developed and no medical advice was available. The women neighbours prescribed that the mother should take glass and grind it to a fine powder with a stone, then lifting the lids she should pour the ground glass into each eye, rubbing it in by diligent massage. The baby would scream, but she should persist, even if the eyes bled freely. The tragedy is that the poor ignorant mother implicitly followed their instructions and blinded her son for life.

In order to arrest haemorrhage, they often plaster the wound with a mixture of cow dung and antimony. This aggravates the lesion, pus accumulates and is unable to escape, and the wound swells and finally bursts. To clean up such a wound before applying a dressing requires boundless patience and skill.

A favourite remedy to reduce inflammation or oedema is cauterisation. A sickle is heated until it is red hot, and the point is then repeatedly applied to the swollen member until the whole area is covered with a series of tiny burns. This remedy is often practised on babies: it is reputed to make them strong! At times a red hot needle is pushed right into the skin and flesh, and a piece of unsterilised string is then pulled through and left in position to act as a drain.

At the mosque in Hammam the boys learn the Koran from wooden slates which are coated with whiting or chalk. The chapter of the Koran which is to be memorised is copied on to the slate with a pen made from a split reed. This is dipped in ink made from charred sheep's wool and gum. When the boys wash off their slates, the water is kept in a large earthen jar outside the mosque. It is called 'Holy water' and is reputed to be a certain remedy for many complaints! The patients drink it, and this, of course, is equivalent to drinking the Word of God!

To cure indigestion or dyspepsia a man is grasped by the throat and throttled until his face turns blue and he becomes unconscious. Dizziness often accompanies anaemia, and this is cured by tying the patient's ankles together, and then suspending him, or her, head down-wards from the central beam of the house. The patient is left in this position for an hour or more. A certain cure for the common cold is to drink a gill of paraffin! When a mother-to-be has been in labour for some time, delivery is hastened by rolling a heavy log over her abdomen, or by a woman jumping on her tummy.

Eye troubles abound. Native doctors operate in a crude way for cataract. They incise the eye ball, and extract the cataract like a pea. In some fifty per cent of the cases the operation succeeds. In many areas almost the whole population suffers from trachoma, or granular lids. This often leads to ingrowing eyelashes. The continual friction of the lashes against the eyeball irritates the eye and eventually leads to opacity of the cornea, and blindness.

One patient was suffering from corneal ulcers. He came to me with a most peculiar contraption over his head. The Arab doctor had treated him for ingrowing eye lashes. The outside skin of the upper eyelids had been compressed between two small pieces of stick. These had been tightly bound together by thread. This caused the skin of the lid to slough away, subsequently scar tissue was formed, so that the eye lashes were drawn away from the cornea. While undergoing this treatment the patient's eyes were kept open by pieces of string tied over his head to a sort of collar round his neck. He had been unable to close his eyes for a month, and corneal ulcers had developed. The principle was good, but the means taken were cruel in the extreme, and involved terrible suffering.

In the early days of our service, smallpox was very prevalent, especially in the more isolated villages. In one place about thirty men and boys gathered on the village square, all afflicted with purulent smallpox. As the message was given, rain started to fall. The men were covered from head to foot with large festering sores and many of them were in the grip of a violent fever. Their wounds were covered with swarms of flies, and those who were strong enough to do so attempted to drive them away with a swatter made from a cow's tail. As I talked with them the flies swarmed all over my face. Suddenly a voice called from a nearby hut, 'Father, come and help me. Take me to be cured.' They carried out a twelve year old boy on his pallet. He was a frightful sight. The sores over his whole body were confluent and had formed a purulent mass. Flies swarmed to and fro. He pleaded to be cured. What could be done? It was too late to help, and soon he and others would pass into eternity. I gave them the few simple remedies that I had with me, and told them the good news in all its simplicity. For the first time in their lives, and for most of them the last time, these men and boys heard the message of eternal life, a hope after death, and of the love of God who forgives. The poor women were just left in the houses to suffer and die. No one cared for them.

It may well be that the reader is filled with revulsion by merely reading about these things. But a servant of God moving about among the people is continually brought face to face with such filth and suffering, so much of which is caused by ignorance and lack of hygiene. If he did nothing to help relieve them he would be almost inhuman. He brings the message of salvation for the soul, but he must do all that he can to relieve their suffering bodies.

For the first few months treatment was given in the garage, but this very soon proved to be inadequate. Crowds flocked to the newly opened dispensary. The news went round very quickly,

'Free medicine.' 'People get better quickly.'

'This new doctor fears God. He prays for us and with us. God heals us.'

'I went to him and it was there that I met God. God spoke to me there.'

'He does not turn any away. You go and see . . .'

So quickly did the news circulate, and so rapidly did numbers increase, that the supply of medicines was quickly exhausted and we had no money to buy more. There was only one thing to do; tell our heavenly Father. So I bowed in prayer and placed the need before the one who never fails. The postman's knock surprised me, for letters were only delivered once a week in this Arab village, and this was not the day for mail. The letter bore the postmark of Torquay, and contained a gift of ten pounds for the medical work—a princely sum at that time. Although I knew no one at Torquay, my Father did, and he had placed the need on the heart of this unknown donor. 'Before they call, I will answer.' I never found who sent it, and never heard from Torquay again!

Weeks passed by; once more supplies were short. I made out an order and addressed it to a wholesale firm of chemists in Algiers. I hesitated to place it in the post, for there was no money in hand; nothing with which to foot the bill. I left for market and when I returned found a letter waiting for me. Again there was a gift for the purchase of medicines. There was enough to pay the bill, plus the carriage from Algiers . . . and one half-penny over.

The people appreciated this work so much that they placed a room at our disposal at a very nominal rent. Twice weekly a clinic was held in this large upper room over a coffee house. It was conveniently situated near the Baths, and yet quite detached, with the door giving on to a yard where the women could wait. Let us take a glance at this place and imagine a typical morning's work. Leaving home at seven o'clock, I reach the out-station in ten minutes to find a crowd of some forty or fifty patients waiting. Some have travelled since the early hours of the morning, leaving their homes in the night to arrive on time. The floor of the room is covered with rough mats, and several benches have been arranged in order to seat the maximum number in the limited space. The women come in first and take the back seats, where they will not be seen, arranging themselves so that just one eye is visible beneath their veils. For many of them it is the only outing that they will have during the whole year—their annual bath! The men then fill up the remainder of the available space, and the meeting begins. I read the story of the paralysed man from Luke 5, and illustrate the message with flannelgraph; emphasising the phrase, 'Son, thy sins be forgiven thee.' Then the truth is pressed home that 'without the shedding of blood there is no forgiveness.' The story of the crucifixion follows. They follow the message intently. One man unconsciously rises to his feet. 'Sit down' his friends shout at him. 'I do not want to miss a word he says,' says the man. Then I pray in the name of the Lord Jesus, asking his blessing on the message, and his healing touch on the sick. How deeply affecting to see these dear Muslims holding out their hands with palms extending upwards during the prayer. This attitude of prayer, copied from believers of Old Testament days, indicates that they desire to receive the blessing asked for in the name of the Lord Jesus. The prayer concludes. There are many loud 'amens', and some kiss their fingers; and then slowly stroke their chins and their chests with their hands. The testimony of one poor 'shut-in' woman given years after was: 'If ever in my life I met God, it was in that dispensary.'

The message ended, the treatment of the men begins. Says the first man, 'I had my whole body covered with a very bad skin disease. It lasted for twelve years. I went to many doctors in France, and in every large city in Algeria, but all the treatment failed until I came to you. Now I am completely healed. God is with you. I believe in the Lord Jesus. I have brought these three men from my village. We left home at three o'clock this morning to come to you.'

The next man has severe malaria, and an injection of

quinine is given. Another suffers from severe indigestion. Each day his friends have almost stangled him in their well-intentioned efforts to cure him. A good purge and a dose of sodium bicarbonate soon puts him right! A case of conjunctivitis is followed by a man with acute bronchitis. He strips to the waist while I examine him with a stethescope, and give him a dose of *Mist: Expect:* from the stock bottle. One after the other the men and boys are treated. The women wait behind. The men are not allowed to look around in curiosity to see who is there! It is 'eyes front,' and those who do not conform are asked to leave.

When the last man has been treated and left, the door is shut and bolted, the veils come off, and treatment of the ladies proceeds. The first is a lady who has eaten nothing for five days. She is white and emaciated. Rising during the night to drink from a pitcher, she had swallowed a horse leech in the water, and the horrible creature had attached itself firmly to the back of her throat behind the nose. The body of the leech is just discernible like a big black swollen slug sucking away at her very life's blood. All efforts to dislodge it had failed, and the poor women is daily growing weaker through loss of blood. With the aid of a pair of artery forceps and a tongue depressor, the leech is removed, a styptic is applied and the haemorrhage is arrested. The poor woman is intensely grateful. Her husband will be too; a new wife costs a lot of money!

The next woman holds a baby in her arms and throws back the shawl. The baby screams as the mother removes a filthy blood-stained rag from its head. She explains that she had left the baby for a moment in its cot, and had run in to speak to the next door neighbour. Snow covered the ground, the door was open, and to keep baby warm she had suspended the cot just near the open fire. The baby, a lovely little girl wrapped in tight swaddling clothes, had wriggled and wriggled and eventually had fallen head first into the fire. The hair was almost completely burned away, together with a large part of the scalp and skin. The bones of the scalp shine through the mass of tar-like substance that has been plastered on it. (This case looked absolutely hopeless. The mother refused to allow the child to go to hospital. However, patient and persistent care triumphed, meningitis did not develop, and the baby lived to become a delightful girl, even although she must always wear a head scarf, being quite bald. There are no wigs in the Kabyle mountains!)

The next patient is a woman with an axillary abscess which should have been excised days ago. Taking all possible precautions, the abscess is opened, the pus drained into a bowl and a dressing applied. Then a tooth is extracted, a case of malaria treated, and a dozen children with suppurating eyes dealt with. A mother asks for medicine for her little girl who is almost at death's door with diarrhoea and vomiting. Cases of TB, skin diseases, dysentry and coughs follow. A woman wants treatment for abdominal pains. She is deeply concerned that she has never had a baby.

The last two patients are girls of fourteen, already young women in this land, and soon to be given in marriage. Such girls are only allowed to leave their homes when accompanied by a male relative. He is waiting outside, and they are now in the care of an old woman who will see that the girls do not misbehave. They take off their veils. What a sight they are. Conjunctivitis has been neglected, and they dread the light. Trachoma has developed. If this is not treated the disease will go on to cause opacity of the cornea and eventual blindness. Their eyes are very swollen and painful. Already there is a white skin growing over the centre of each eye. They receive treatment, and take away ointment and eye drops for use at home. They must return twice a week for treatment for a considerable time. This really pleases them, for they are glad to escape from the seclusion of their homes for a few hours. We pray that through regular attendance at the meetings the light of the glorious gospel may shine into their sin-blinded hearts.

Now nearly fifty others wait their turn outside. They have waited for three hours already. The European doctor has meanwhile been down with his beautifully equipped mobile clinic, offering immediate and free treatment to all who will avail themselves of it. He has had six patients and left.

'Hurry up, sheikh.' 'We left home early this morning and travelled for more than four hours to get here.'

'The doctor was available. Why did you not go to him? Treatment is free there as it is here.'

'Sheikh, we know that you love us, we trust you, and above all, you fear God. You pray for us and with us. You tell us about God. That is why we come to you, but these two veiled women who have come with me are getting tired of waiting.'

Once more the room is filled to capacity; the men in front and the women behind. Another message from the Bible, prayer, and treatment is resumed. The first patient has a dislocated jaw. He has walked for four hours and has nothing to eat for three days. He can only mumble and is in great pain.

'Give him a sharp blow on the chin, sheikh,' says one man. I put him in a chair in the corner where his head is immobilised, wrap a towel round my thumbs on each hand, remembering the instructions given at Livingstone College long ago. Grasping the man's lower jaw firmly I exert steady pressure downward, then back, round and up. With a click the jaw slips back into place. A murmur of approval goes up from the other patients.

'May God be merciful to your forefathers.'

'May he give you many more children, and multiply your family.'

'May God bless you and give you many good things.'
The man gently feels his jaw, moves it up and down, and a big grin spreads over his face! Next patient,

please. So the work goes on.

'Hit me with a needle, I have fever.'

'I have a frog in my throat,' complains another.

'My tummy goes up and down like this, and then round and round like this,' says one old man, demonstrating with his hands.

'Listen to the worms moving in my tummy,' says another and he allows to listen to the gurgle!

Again the men have all been treated and left. The ladies remain, and most of them are young. Many have some sort of feminine abdominal trouble. One old lady seems to be in great pain. She hobbles to the front. 'I was feeding the mule, when it stepped back and trod on my toe,' she said. The mule had trodden so hard that the toe was almost severed. It was quite easy to amputate it, to apply a dressing and bandage. In a Kabyle house, where the animals share a limited space with human beings such accidents often happen.

On one occasion, having cared for over a hundred patients single-handed, and given two messages in Arabic, I felt completely exhausted.

'I will care for those of you who remain,' I said to the men. 'I will just give you medicine, but I feel too tired to give a message from God's Word.'

'But why do you think that we come to you instead of going to the *tebib*?' they said. 'It is only because you fear God and ask him to heal us and he does. If there is no message, sheikh, then you must at least pray with us in the name of the Lord Jesus.' Tired though I was, I felt that I must accede to their request and give a short message, perhaps the last they would ever hear.

Through the medical work I often obtained an insight into the private lives of the people, enabling me to better understand their customs, the bondage of the women, and the superstitions which dominate their lives. I was often helped in this way to make the gospel relevant to their needs and circumstances.

One old man of over eighty years of age was found to

have taken a new wife every year in a vain attempt to have children, and to prevent his name and family from becoming extinct. Many of these wives had been young girls. At the time he had two wives, one a girl of four-teen. Only financial reasons kept him from taking the four wives that are allowed to every Muslim, with as many concubines as he can support. This old man must have had at least sixty consecutive wives, but it was all in vain. There were no children.

The more ignorant people always seek a quick cure. They will sometimes drink a whole bottle full of medi-cine at one draught. Why spread it over a week when you can drink it all and be cured at once? One man sent his little daughter for medicine. He was suffering from a violent headache and severe fever. The French have a lotion that they call *Eau Sedative*, and the older people appreciate this, as it often quickly relieves their headaches. I gave the girl a few tablets of asprin, a purge and a bottle of *Eau Sedative*, with strict instruc-tions as to how each was to be used. The man decided that he must get better in the shortest possible time. He swallowed all the tablets and the two pills, washing them down with all the lotion. The next day he was completely cured! The Muslim is a born fatalist. One of the best known words in his language is *mektoub* (It is decreed). He will defer treatment till the last possible moment, hoping against hope for a cure. If he recovers it is *mektoub*, and if he dies, it is God who has decreed it.

Perhaps the women suffer more than the men because of this fatalistic attitude, this unwillingness to seek advice and treatment. 'Sheikh, have you anything in your bag to help my wife? She is feeding a baby, but one breast is four times the size of the other. Please come and see her.' Normally I did not carry drugs or medicines with me, but I always took a scalpel and one or two other instruments. The poor woman was suffer-ing terribly. She had not slept for nights because of the pain. The breast was distended to many times its normal size, the whole organ was tense, the axillary glands swollen. The woman was running a high temperature, and there was a very real danger of septicaemia. The only thing to do was to incise the abscess. Preparing the scalpel, I stood behind the poor woman and plunged it in. With a scream she darted away, completing the job. The abscess was well and truly opened! The confined pus spurted out and hit the roof. The cleaning-up process was exceedingly painful, for the adjacent sections of the breast were infected, and had to be broken down for the pus to be drawn off. I dressed the wound, gave her a sedative, and before I left she had fallen sound asleep. The next day she came over to the clinic for further treatment. Rushing into the room after her long journey, she pulled down my head, and covered me with kisses! Then she grasped the hand that had held the scalpel, and kissed that time and again. Her gratitude was boundless. The treatment was crude, but efficacious, and she was so grateful.

Back at home, I spent the afternoon preparing stock medicines for the next session at the clinic, for I was not only doctor and nurse, but chemist, dispenser and dentist. Teeth were extracted at any time—a man or woman suffering from severe toothache cannot be made to wait several days. One day there was a knock at our front door. Pearl opened it to see a man with a very swollen jaw who was obviously in great pain, standing outside. Very timidly he asked, 'Is the sheikh at home? I want him to take my tooth out.' 'I am so sorry, but he is in the villages, and will not be back till night.' 'Praise God for that!' said the man, walking away with evident relief.

'Such a fellow deserves to be treated in the same way that he treats the nationals', says a critic. 'How would he like to have a tooth extracted without an anaesthetic?' Yes, it does us all good to have a taste of our own medicine!

It happened during the Second World War when the Germans were patrolling Algeria. There was no petrol for cars, travelling was almost impossible. Cars were laid up. I suddenly developed severe toothache. A few days before I had tried to open an abscess on my own arm, but failed. I looked at the tooth in a mirror. It was a large molar. Could I possibly extract it myself? I had done this with a root, but a molar? I decided that I must put myself in the capable hands of my dear wife who was a nurse. To be sure, she had never before extracted a tooth, although I had had to operate on her. Now was her chance to get her own back. I gave her very detailed instructions. She put me in a chair in the corner where my head was held by the two walls. Escape was impossible. 'Now apply the forceps, press them well down to get a grip of the roots. Gently ease it from its socket and pull.' It sounded so simple, but there was no anaesthetic. She made an excellent job of that first extraction, but continued the rocking process slightly longer than was necessary.' Pull, pull,' I shouted. Out it came, and the only unprofessional touch was that the dentist and not the patient burst into a flood of tears. I am sure that I showed far more sympathy with the next patient who came for tooth extraction—it happened to be the European doctor!

One of the most effective weapons in spiritual warfare is Christian love expressed in a practical way. Strange indeed that a man's respect and confidence can be won by extracting his tooth; or the appreciation of a woman gained by opening an abscess. Yet so it is. Suspicions are allayed, the love of Christ is seen in action—the bigoted spirit of a fanatical man is changed to a friendly receptive attitude. Thus in hundreds of villages I was welcomed and my message received, and the patients carried the message that they had heard over a very wide area—as far as the Sahara.

Chapter Five

Discipleship: Counting the Cost

One of the strongest proofs of the reality of Christianity is the amazing courage of converts from Islam who face ostracism, blows and continual persecution for Christ's sake.

Abd Allah seemed loth to leave the men's meeting, although it was already ten o'clock at night. The message that evening had affected him deeply. He was obviously impressed, but could not bring himself to decide for Christ. 'No,' he said 'It's hard, too hard for me.' I replied, 'Surely you have not yet understood how easy it is to become a Christian. The Lord Jesus died on the cross to give you eternal life, and you simply trust him to save you. He did it all. He finished the work, and you have only to accept him as your Lord and Saviour.'

'Yes, I know. It is easy. *It is easy . . . for you*, but it is *hard for us.* So very hard,' he said.

What did this Muslim man mean? He continued, 'Think of all that I must face if I become a Christian. I am thirty-five years of age, and still live in my father's house. I work for him. As head of our house he sells the figs and oil and wheat and takes the money. With it he buys the food for us all. We all live in one courtyard. We have our meals together. If I do become a Christian he will disinherit me and turn me from his home. My wife comes from a very fanatical Muslim family, and she would immediately leave me. I should have to bring up my four children alone. I could not re-marry, because a Christian is permitted to have only one wife, and I could not divorce my present wife. I should be virtually alone and homeless, and even if I did find another room or house in which to live, I should be surrounded by Muslims. That means that I should be compelled to contribute to the support of the village sheikh, who is of course a Muslim. When my daughters grow old enough to marry, no one would want to marry them. They would carry the stigma of being daughters of an infidel. If I sought employment elsewhere, no one would want to employ me in this Muslim land. When the men go to the mosque to pray, I could not join them if I were a Christian. To do so would be to renounce my faith. We live a communal life, but in times of sickness or trouble they would not lift a finger to help me. When trouble came to me, they would rejoice that I was under the curse of God. God would be punishing me for becoming a Christian. Yousef is a Christian, and you know that when his baby died last year no one would help to bury it. Can you imagine his heartbreak? He had to dig the grave himself, and bury his own child, while the Muslims stood by and looked on, scoffing and jeering. That is what I dread most of all; the scoffs and the jeers. They would call me 'an infidel dog'. Every moment of the day I should show that I am a Christian, for I could no longer use the Muslim phrases that enter into every part of our life. I could no longer swear, 'By the great Koran,' or even 'By the truth of God'! I could not use any of the other oaths and phrases that Muslims employ every day of their lives. They would try and turn my mind with secret drugs; and even attempt to poison me. You do not know the power of charms and the occult, but all these things would be used against me. My cousin is a shopkeeper and he would love to be a Christian, but then his shop would be boycotted, no one would buy from an infidel. Only last week I heard of Zouhra. She is only a child, but everyone knows that she loves the Lord Jesus. Do you know that every week when she comes to your classes they throw stones at her as she comes along the street. My children would be made to suffer like that. Yes, sheikh, it *is* easy . . . for you. But it is hard, so hard for us.'

Ali was a regular attender. He was a working man with one child, whom he loved dearly. How intently he listened to the Good News. To him it was as cold water to a thirsty soul. Others noticed his rapt attention, his sympathetic attitude, his serious manner. They decided that at any price he must be turned away from Christ. They told him that a good Muslim would not attend gatherings at which the name of Mohammed was never mentioned. They reminded him that only a week previously a man who attended these very meetings had been called from his home and shot dead on the spot. They were fully aware that this incident had had nothing to do with the men's meeting, but they could use it to frighten Ali. He replied, 'You can stop threatening me, for I shall never stop going to hear about the Lord Jesus. He loved me enough to die for me, and I love him dearly. In fact, I would sooner die, than turn aside from following him.' They were bold words in a Muslim land. Within a few days Ali was desperately ill, and was taken to hospital. Although every effort was made to save his life, he died and went to be with Christ, which is far better; but he left a sorrowing widow and an orphan child. It was not until after his death that Pearl was told by the women neighbours of the threats, of Ali's brave testimony and his determination never to turn aside. They knew, everyone knew, that Ali died as a Christian. It was sad to see his empty seat at the men's meetings. Numbers dwindled. The effect of his death on the work of God was disastrous. So the opposition increased, but we plodded on.

One of the greatest tests for a Christian is the Fast of Ramadhan. Every Muslim is required to observe this; eating and drinking nothing from early morning until sunset, for a whole month. The law of apostasy in Islam declares that whosoever breaks the Fast of Ramadhan is to be regarded as an apostate, and may be legitimately deprived of wealth and life. A female apostate is to be confined in a separate apartment, starved and beaten daily until she returns to the faith of Islam. In present-day Egypt a law is being promulgated which condemns to death any Muslim who becomes a Christian. In Morocco a man who was bold enough to eat during Ramadhan because he was a Christian was sentenced in the lawcourts to nine months' imprisonment.

In a certain Kabyle village, smoke rising from a small house proclaimed to all that a family was defying the law of Islam, the law of apostasy, that is still valid in every Muslim land. Everyone knew that the man and his wife were Christians. He was allowing his wife to prepare food during the day time, and they were both breaking the Fast. He had recently returned from France, where he had enjoyed liberty as a sergeant in the French army. To cook food in an Algerian village was an unforgiveable offence which must be punished. How dare they do such a thing? They must be taught a lesson which would serve to discourage others. Two days later their delightful little babe was brought to my father-in-law, writhing in agony. Every effort to save the little life failed, and the lovely baby died. The next week the wife died, and the week after that the man. To this day, Muslims curse and spit as they pass those three graves. Islam defies your King. It is hard to be a Christian . . . in a Muslim land.

Various methods are employed to bring about death. One of these was discovered quite accidentally. An orphan girl, who had been adopted by missionaries, was afflicted with chronic enteritis. No treatment availed and the child died. Shortly before her death she passed a long hair in the faeces, and suspicions were aroused. Yes, it was foul play. Diligent enquiry elicited the following facts. Hairs are taken from a mule's tail and wound into a tight ball. This is encased in dough and forms a small pellet. The pellet is put into the couscous or berkoukes, which is swallowed without mastication. The dough dissolves in the intestine, the hairs unravel and provoke a chronic inflammation for which there is no cure. A qualified surgeon conducting a post-mortem would not easily detect the cause of the insidious death. Sometimes ground glass is mixed with the food and brings about an even more painful death, and in all such cases it is almost impossible to trace the person responsible. '*Dh-Rebbi* (It is God),' they say.

While men meet with violent opposition, poisoning and death, a woman may have to face continual ostracism and persecution. She is confined to the house, from which escape is impossible, and she has no one to whom she can turn. She is deprived of all Christian fellowship.

Fathem was deeply concerned about her salvation. Her heart was moved to think that the Lord Jesus cared for her enough to die for her. She told her relatives, 'The Lord Jesus died for us all, not only for Europeans.' At once everyone turned against her. They called her a *kafra*, an infidel. She no longer believed in Mohammed, but some doubts still remained in her mind. She could not forget the Word of God, and when Pearl visited her, she used to look around furtively saying, 'Is anyone listening?' She continued to listen, drank in the message and finally committed herself wholly to the Lord Jesus. Then she felt that she could no longer pray as a Muslim, and told her husband so. 'Why not?' he asked. 'Because I am a Christian, and Christians do not pray in that way.' He decided that it must be thrashed out of her, and whipped and beat her unmercifully. He threatened her with divorce. (To divorce her he had only to raise his hand and say, 'You are divorced.' She would then have to leave the house and leave her children, go back to her father, and be given in marriage to a strange man. Her mother-heart yearned for her little ones.)

Then Ramadhan came round. Should a Christian, redeemed by the precious blood of Christ, observe the Fast?' No, so for his sake she ate and drank. Her husband came in and discovered her eating. Again he threatened her with divorce. As he sat in the coffee house drinking coffee, a neighbour taunted him, 'Do you call yourself a man? You allow your wife to eat during Ramadhan? You have no moustaches, no pride.' One day he could stand it no longer. His pride was touched. He would show her and the neighbours who was master. He went home and beat her, compelling her to observe the fast. Her screams and sobs were evidence enough to the neighbours. Now she was shunned even by her friends. They cleared their throats and spat at her whenever they saw her, or even when they passed her house. Her children were stoned and ill-treated because their mother was a hated Christian. She decided that she would continue to believe secretly in her heart. Nothing could change that. 'Why should I continue to suffer like this? I will be a Christian in my heart, but not let others know. God knows my deep, deep longings,' she thought. She prayed. She fasted. Ramadhan was now over, but to please her husband, she fasted to make up for the days that she had missed. She paid the fine imposed for not having fasted for the whole month of Ramadhan. Her love for the Lord grew cold. She even told lies to shield herself, and that deep joy that she had when she first knew the Lord disappeared. Fear and shame turned her back. She is no longer a keen Christian, nor is she a Muslim. Yes, it is hard to be a Christian . . . in a Muslim land.

Waheeba wrote to her friend with whom she had been staying for a few days, 'You know well that I am Christian. The first thing that I did when I reached home was to pray, and then I told my parents. I told them that I could no longer fast during Ramadham. I explained why, and then, all that evening, I assure you, I was hit on every hand. They all hit me. They said, 'You will have to fast.' I said, 'I will fast, but I will not do it with intention. I will fast, but with the intention in my heart to follow Jesus and not to obey Islam.' They said, 'You have betrayed your faith.' Dear friend, I beg of you to help me, for they want to marry me to a Muslim man. I am broken-hearted, and I eat hardly anything. They told me, 'We will throw you out,' I said, 'Yes, but even if you do, I will not deny my Saviour and renounce him.' Everyone is against me. I beg you to find me a shelter in a Christian family. My mother wants only the money she will get when I am sold in marriage to an old man. The younger the girl, the higher the price, and I am only fifteen.' What a choice for a girl only fifteen years old! To be put on the street for a life of shame, or to be forcibly married to a Muslim man.

Basheer was the first Arab boy whom I led to the Lord, and the first to be baptised, the first day that he attended the clinic, he sat among a crowd of men, clad in a ragged burnous which must have been handed down to him from several older brothers. His eyes were swollen and almost closed, and it was only with great pain and difficulty that he could lift his head and look at me. I carefully lifted those lids, and found that the entire cornea of each eye was opaque, covered with a thin white skin. I had seen him two days before in a wretched hovel that he called home. Heavy snow had fallen and cow dung had been piled on the fire in a vain attempt to warm the house. Basheer shivered in the cold. There was no chimney; and the smoke, which blackened the rafters and the walls, irritated those suffering eyes. It was quite clearly a case of neglected trachoma, which, if untreated, would ultimately lead to blindness. He was unable to go to the mosque to learn to read in Arabic, or to attend school.

Nine years of suffering had passed since his birth,

and now he had come for treatment. I gave him some soothing eye lotion and some mercurial ointment, telling him how to use them. On each visit to the clinic I also treated the inverted lids. In five months there was a great improvement. He was able to attend the weekly class for boys, and also started to go to the mosque to learn to read in Arabic.

Pearl used to visit Basheer's mother every week. She was a Kabyle and listened eagerly to the New Testament in her mother tongue. There was no doubt in her mind that this message of life was for her. Cost what it might, she must give open expression to her new found faith. 'What has Mohammed done for us women? He has dragged us down, crushed us as grain in a mortar, and cowed and beaten us like this.' She illustrated her words by violently thumping her hand with her clenched fist.

'Since trusting the Lord Jesus I have been blessed in every way. I have finished with all this superstition.' She took the charms from round her neck and flung them into the open fire. Thus she made a clean break with the past. Fathema was a Christian.

It was a terrible thing in the eyes of the Muslims for a high class Marabout woman like her to confess faith in the Lord Jesus. Troubles soon began. Their only cow mysteriously died. Then one by one their goats died. Miriam the youngest daughter appeared to be dominated by an evil spirit. She was demented and finally died. Catastrophe after catastrophe fell on the family. It was as if all the powers of the evil one were unleashed. Every one was such a blow to Fathema. How much she looked forward to the weekly visits. She could confide in Pearl, and knew that she was utterly worthy of her confidence. Basheer had started attending the class for boys. Although he could not read, he quickly learned some Scriptures by heart, and it was not long before he trusted the Saviour. The other members of the family were totally opposed. It was impossible for either Basheer or his mother to pray openly. Each night Basheer would creep into his mother's bed, and pulling the blanket over their heads, it became a little sanctuary where they could pray together in the precious name of the Lord Jesus. Fathema learned so much from her son as he repeated the lessons he had heard in the classes.

One day, when the men had gathered in the dispensary, and the meeting was in progress, I quoted two verses of the Bible that Basheer had learned by heart. 'Christ died for our sins according to the Scriptures, he was buried and he rose again, according to the Scriptures,' and, 'The blood of Jesus Christ, his Son, cleanses us from all sin.' The boy's voice rang out loud and clear as he also repeated the texts. 'That is what I believe in my heart. I believe that Jesus died for me.' What looks of hatred were focussed on him! *'Wa ma qatalu hu wa ma salabu hu,'* repeated one. ('They did not kill him, they did not crucify him.') 'I believe that he died for me,' insisted Basheer. But he was only a boy, and nearly blind. Let his family deal with him! They let it pass.

At this time we went to England for our first furlough, and Pearl was unable to visit Fathema. Basheer and his mother were alone. 'Now is the time to scare this fearless woman who claims to be a Christian,' thought the head man of the village. 'I will teach her a lesson that she will never forget, and openly expose her as a Christian.' She was a distant relative of his, bearing the same name, so that at times he had access to her house. 'If you do not renounce your faith in Jesus Christ, and give some outward evidence that you are still a Muslim, I will disgrace you before all. Give us proof that you do believe in Mohammed. Pray openly, witness to Mohammed, buy some more charms containing verses of the Holy Koran, and wear them, or else you will see what we do to an apostate woman like you.' Fathema was terrified. She knew that they were not just empty words. To whom could she turn? There was no one, no one except her Lord, and to him she poured out her heart.

Two days later an old woman came in. 'Muwatata, have you heard the news? The head man is dead.' It seemed almost incredible that that tall strong man in the prime of life should have suddenly been struck down by God. 'Listen, you can hear the wailing of the women. They are to bury him today.' Could it be possible? The man who had threatened to expose her, to illtreat her because she was a Christian, and who was so determined to make her recant, was dead! She was safe. More than that, everyone would see that this was the hand of God.

Fathema was more than ever convinced of the power of the Lord Jesus. When Pearl returned from furlough Fathema said, 'I made sure that you had abandoned me for ever, and had forgotten me. But the Lord Jesus never left me. He is with me here in this little hut. I am more than ever convinced that he alone is the way to God.' What a tremendous encouragement this was to Basheer. God had vindicated his mother's faith. He decided that he too would follow—all the way.

The classes continued and each week nearly thirty boys attended. The Muslim sheikh listed the names of all those attending. At any cost this must be stopped! Two sturdy fellows were called in to help him. One by one the boys were taken to the mosque by these bigger boys who roughly threw each boy to the ground. These were boys who were in danger of becoming Christians. Their ankles were bound tightly together, and the soles of their feet lifted in the air by one big boy, while the other applied the *bastinado*. They yelled, they screamed and struggled, but all in vain. Not until twenty five strokes had been well and truly applied were they released. Then with swollen blistered feet they dragged themselves away. Basheer came in for a special share of the torture. 'We will teach you to be Christians.

It is strictly forbidden in a Muslim land.'

The next week Basheer came to the class surreptitiously, cautiously. Was anyone looking? He was so afraid, but he came . . . alone.

The years went by, and we moved back to Lafayette. Each Sunday morning there was a meeting for Christians. It meant a long journey on foot for Basheer and his friend to attend. Basheer was now a lad of fifteen, and boys of that age are obliged to keep the fast of Ramadhan. His brother Belhaj knew that Basheer would stay for dinner with us after the meeting, even though it was Ramadhan. Why should he allow this young brother to dishonour the family in this way? He decided to teach Basheer a lesson that he would never forget.

Arming himself with a stout cudgel, Belhaj hid behind a rock, waiting for the two boys to come down the road. He was well away from the village, so that any screams would be unheard and unheeded. He sprang out on them and caught his brother. The stick fell on the weak boy's back with sickening thuds. 'Take that . . . and that. Remember . . . I will teach you to break the Fast, to disobey me!' Basheer fell to the ground unconscious; but Belhaj continued to rain blow after blow on his poor frail body. He regained consciousness and pleaded for mercy, but without avail. At last his brother's anger abated. He partly carried and partly drove the poor lad back to the village, driving him on with more blows. He dragged him to the mosque and there the sheikh added his quota of blows.

At last Basheer was released and dragged himself painfully home. His mother spread the mat and made his bed, tenderly covering him with blankets. He was in the throes of fever. Pneumonia developed. His mother was sure that he would die, but she encouraged him; 'God has still work for you to do, my son. He will not let you die.' How his poor body ached. Where was his friend the missionary? Why did he not come? Surely someone would tell him what had happened. I was not told until ten days later. When I did see Basheer the poor lad was covered from head to foot with bruises, his whole body was black and blue. He recovered, but his constitution was shaken, and a little later that winter he became ill with pneumonia. His mother asked Belhaj to come and tell me so that I could care for my brother in Christ, but Belhaj was adamant. 'May God curse him, and the religion of his forefathers! May he strike him blind! I would rather see my brother die than go to a Christian for help.'

The following year Basheer decided that he would not provoke his brother by staying at home during Ramadhan. He made his home in a little watchman's hut in the garden by the river, where he could watch the vegetables and cucumbers. The rats were his only companions. He could nibble cucumbers and pomegranates and in this way God knew he had broken the Fast. Once more his brother found him and beat him. Basheer then travelled thirty miles on foot to his mother's relations in Kabylia. There he stayed until the Fast had ended.

'It is the happiest day of my life,' said Basheer when he was baptised. He was now eighteen and at last a man, able to choose for himself. What a victory it was for the Lord. 'At last I have been able to obey my Lord,' he said. In order to shield him, and one other woman who was baptised at the same time, we had made a baptistry in our hall. Basheer had helped me to dig out the earth. 'I feel as if I were digging my own grave', he said. How well these converts from Islam understand the meaning of baptism as total identification with Christ in his death and burial. From then on he was present every Sunday at the worship meeting, and it was like music to listen to him as he praised the Lord.

Nine months later I was once more called to his home. I was dismayed to see his emaciated body, his huge distended abdomen; to hear of the violent pains, and uncontrollable dysentric symptoms. I did my very best to care for the poor boy. It was during the days of the Second World War when we had no petrol, and every car was off the road. Very few medicines were available. Every effort to save Basheer's life failed. He went to be with his Lord, just nine months after his baptism. 'If any man follow me, let him take up his cross.' It is hard to be a Christian . . . in a Muslim land.

Chapter Six

This Woman whom Satan has Bound

When a baby girl is born her arms are placed by her side, her feet are put together and then the whole body is wound round with dirty rags, leaving just the feet showing. The cradle is a very primitive affair, and swings from a beam in the roof. There are very few bed clothes, and the baby is effectively immobilised by the swaddling clothes. In this way she will spend the first months of her life, unable to throw off the blanket or to move about. Before a Muslim woman is buried her body is washed, after which sixteen yards of material are wound tightly round it. Thus the body is bound before burial. What an apt picture this is of a Muslim woman's life, bound from birth to death! We read in the Gospels of a woman whom Satan had bound for eighteen years; but who was liberated by the power of the Lord Jesus. The enemy of souls holds millions of Muslim women and girls captive by means of cruel customs which originated with, and are perpetuated by, Islam, and which blight and blast, degrade and debase their lives.

Careful observation over many years has confirmed the impression that in North Africa there are many women who are devout Christians. In their zeal and love for the Lord, their devotion to his Word and their deep desire to win others for him, they often surpass the men, but Satan ensures that their sphere of in-

fluence and witness shall be strictly limited. They have
certainly found liberty in Christ, but the restrictions
imposed on women by custom and cruelty ensure that
their sphere of witness is limited to one small corner.
This is one of the ways in which Satan works in Muslim
lands.

'Come and see our little baby boy, sheikh. He is very
ill and I am afraid that evil spirits have taken possession
of him, and made him blind.' Baby had been born a day
or two previously, after five days of suffering for the
poor girl-mother. It was her first baby and she was only
a child herself. The birth had been protracted, so that
Kabyle midwives had crowded round and used every
possible means to effect a delivery. A heavy piece of
wood had been rolled over the mother's abdomen to
help expel the child. Now she was weak, and longed to
be left to sleep, but she was not allowed to do so. She
must keep her eyes fixed on her little son all day long
for fear the evil spirits should take him away, and sub-
stitute a spirit child. Whenever she dozed off she was
roughly shaken, and told to watch her child. She longed
for a drink of water, but this was denied her, lest the
water should make her stomach swell. She was given
olive oil and eggs to help her milk. The shrill cries of the
women, and the continual clapping of hands made
sleep impossible. As usual, there was great rejoicing
because the baby was a boy. Guns were fired, and the
women pierced the air with their 'You-yous' and shouts
of joy. Had it been a girl there would have been no such
rejoicings. Baby is never washed in water, but just
smeared in oil, rubbed with salt and then wrapped in
swaddling clothes. When the eyes swell and become in-
flamed it is attributed to the influence of evil spirits,
and not to lack of cleanliness.

Some girls are allowed their freedom until they are
fourteen years of age, and in independent Algeria,
an increasing number of girls are allowed to go to
school, especially in the towns. At any time they may be

shut away, and this often happens when they are only twelve years old. The deciding factor is not age, but physical development, and the reason is that immorality is rife in Muslim lands. The punishment for immorality in Kabylia is death for the woman, especially when an unmarried girl becomes preganant. She has brought dishonour on the family. When a girl is shut in, she is confined to her one-roomed house, and is no longer allowed to go out at will. Her studies come to an end. She may be permitted to go into the courtyard, but woe betide her if she is found peeping out at passers-by in the road. If ever she is allowed out, she must be closely veiled and accompanied by a male relative or an old woman. Such a girl is occassionally allowed out to go to the public baths, to see a doctor or, on very rare occasions, to go to a wedding. A young woman never goes out for a walk, or does her own shopping. The man of the house brings in the food from the market, and her clothes from the local shops. More freedom is permitted to girls in the towns than in the country districts and more restrictions are imposed on better class girls than on their poorer counterparts.

A girl may be given in marriage as early as twelve. She does not see her future husband before the wedding, and she has no choice in the matter at all. She must go to the man chosen for her by her father or brother. He may be older than her father, and may possibly already have three other wives. She is then the man's darling for a short time, and is petted and spoiled, but soon becomes, as the youngest wife, the drudge of the household. If a girl's father is absent from home, her uncle or older brother has the right to sell her in marriage to the man he chooses; and that is generally to the highest bidder. 'You may make of your wife anything you like, except a corpse,' runs the proverb. 'Marriage is a kind of slavery, in which man is the master,' wrote one of their learned, holy men. Child marriage is still common, though forbidden by law. It has the highest authority; for the prophet married Ayesha at the age of six, and they co-habited when she was only nine years old. She was his wife for nine years. Oh the unspeakable sadness of the lives of many of these poor women and girls! In all fairness it must be said that in the towns conditions are rapidly improving. The girls are fighting for more liberty, and the abolition of the veil. Both fellows and girls are demanding to see their partners before marriage. The law of the land makes it illegal for a girl to be given in marriage under the age of sixteen, or without her consent, but such laws are often flouted. An increasing number of girls are going on to higher education, and some are completing their studies at Universities, but many a broken heart and thwarted life is to be found in the inland villages.

A young girl will often become successively the wife of four or five men before ultimately settling with her permanent husband. A woman may be divorced at any time at the whim of her husband. She has no choice but to leave, and that means saying farewell to her children, leaving everything and returning to her father. The man has simply to raise his hand and say, 'You are divorced,' and she must go. If he repeats the formula three times she cannot return to him until she has spent at least one night with another man. When divorced she must hand over her children to the care of another woman and never see them again. As often as not, the one who replaces her is a girl-wife who could not care less for the babies and children of her predecessor. A married woman never takes the name of her husband, but retains her maiden name throughout her life. The biggest tragedy is that a woman of thirty-five who has already born sixteen or more babies has become in the eyes of her husband an old woman. He divorces her, she is worth very little, and her father sells her to an old man, and her real husband takes a girl wife. Every year many girls from our Sunday School classes were married to men who had divorced their wives. It is this that condemns Islam even more than the fact that it allows polygamy.

In one village, I arrived at the house where I was to spend the night in time for them to prepare a meal for me. I sat with my host on the mat and his wife brought in a lovely bowl of couscous on which she had placed a nice fat chicken. She had carefully prepared the couscous, made the soup, and it was a delicious meal. Her husband had not consulted her, but had caught her chicken, cut its throat and told her to prepare the meal. Now he broke the chicken into pieces with his hands, giving me a leg and part of the breast, and taking a similar portion for himself. The remainder was handed to his sons who ate with us. His wife hovered round in the background, almost unseen. The meal finished, he called to her to take away the remains. She had to be content with the couscous that was left, and the neck and claws. These were her portion. Yet, that chicken was the only thing that she could really call her own, apart from her cheap jewelry. She had continually denied herself scraps of food to feed it, and the eggs that it produced were hers. She could sell them and use the money for herself, the only money that she ever had. She was not asked to give the chicken. It was just taken. She could have the neck and the claws. A trivial incident, yet a straw which shows how the current flows.

Nevertheless, it would be wrong to picture all Muslim women and girls as desperately unhappy. In fact, the reverse is often the case, for they hide their sorrows. In country districts some women have much more liberty than those in towns. They can move freely in the courtyard of their homes. On market day, when the men are all away from the village, they can flit from house to house along the village street or slip away to the fountain. The poorer women in Kabyle villages are sometimes allowed to go to work in the fields, or to gather olives. It is the woman who grinds the corn, sifts the meal, and makes the bread and couscous. She takes the wool from the sheep's back, washes the fleece, spins it into yarn. Then she sets up the loom and makes brightly coloured blankets, or the white seamless burnous worn by the men. The blankets are wonderfully woven with beautiful intricate designs.

Every part of a woman's life is linked with fertility, and so the designs on the blankets depict the fields, the running water, the scales on the serpents back, the whole taking one's mind back to the garden of Eden. The fertility of the fields is thought to be very closely linked with that of the home. The blankets depict this. It is the woman who tends the animals, and milks the cows and the goats. She plasters the walls of the house within and without, and whitewashes them. She moulds the pottery and bakes it in the courtyard; sometimes ornamenting it with artistic patterns of her own design. The men do all the sewing and embroidery, although an increasing number of women are getting sewing machines, and now make the dresses for the girls and women of their village. Formerly it was the village tailor who did this.

Fear is always the controlling element in the life of a woman. She is always under the domination of a man. From early childhood her brothers are encouraged to beat her and illtreat her. When still a child she is taught to fear the power of evil spirits, and talismans and charms are hung round her neck. When married she is subject to her husband, who compels her to carry out his every whim. The fear of divorce hangs over her head like the sword of Damocles. She fears the autocratic mother-in-law; for it is she who controls the whole household. When young the mother-in-law has been made to suffer, and she will see to it that her daughter-in-law suffers as much as, or more than, she did. She tells her son about the defects and shortcomings of his wife, and encourages him to beat her.

When there is a co-wife each is afraid of the other; afraid that she will plot against her, so that her husband will turn her out. She is afraid of the gossiping tongues of the old women who go from house to house and spread trouble, separating husband and wife. When her baby is born she fears the neighbours who will come in and covet it. A neighbour will enter the house and say, 'What a lovely baby.' She looks at the child with the evil eye. The poor baby soon refuses to eat, becomes sick, wizens and dies. They say that the demons have taken the true child and replaced it with a demon child. Above all, there is the fear of death and the hereafter, for many believe that women have no place in heaven. She shows this fear even in her devotions. It is fear that compels her to pray, to fast and to witness to Mohammed. She bows down to Allah, and takes the abject attitude of a slave prostrating herself before a hard master. They know nothing of the love of God as shown in the Lord Jesus; that perfect love which casts out fear. For the girls or women who do trust the Lord Jesus there is the continual fear of evil tongues, of threatened divorce, of poisoning or drugs, of whippings or beatings, and of every form of ill treatment. 'This woman whom Satan has bound' so adequately portrays their lives. Only Christ can free them, giving spiritual liberty, yet many must remain to the end of their earthly life in physical and moral bondage.

Chapter Seven

World Wide War—
The Work Continues

The clouds of war hung ominously over Europe in September 1939. We were on holiday at Djidjelli with our two children when a telegram arrived late one night intimating that some of our friends were leaving for England in thirty six hours. It would probably be the last opportunity for our daughter Daisy to leave the country before the outbreak of war. Early next morning we called her into our bedroom and put the position clearly before her. Would she rather stay with us and share the isolation of Algeria, or leave home to go to school in England? God alone knows the heart searchings, the deep sorrow, and the cost to each of us of that decision. War was declared soon after her arrival in England, France fell, and when next we saw our lovely daughter, she was a strapping girl of fourteen. After four and a half years of separation she hardly knew us, and we scarcely knew her. God in his grace honoured the decision, and for more than twenty five years, Daisy has been a missionary to the Kabyles. For many years she continued to work alone in Algeria, on a mission station which had been previously staffed by six people. This was followed by a period in France; and years of broadcasting with her voice being used in the conversion of scores of Muslims.

When France fell in 1940, we were cut off from all financial support emanating from England. Prices immediately soared, the shops emptied, and it was virtually impossible to purchase articles of clothing or medical supplies. Total monthly rations were ½lb of sugar, 3 oz of ersatz coffee, ½lb of soap, 4 oz of paraffin, and ½lb of black bread each day. Our clothing ration was one yard per person per year! Everything else had to be bought at black market prices. Milk, butter, cheese, margerine and jam were unobtainable. It was at this time that God gave us another baby girl who arrived just ten years after her brother. Normally a letter from England took only a few days, but all postal communications with the homeland were severed. Could we trust God to supply at such a time?

Years before, a Roman Catholic family had attended the French gospel services. Father, mother, daughter and grand-daughter were all deeply affected by the message, but made no open profession of conversion. They had subsequently left and moved rightaway to another part of Algeria. We had completely forgotten them. Then one day we received this letter:

> Dear Friends, France has fallen. We understand that you are now cut off from all financial supplies from the United Kingdom. Please feel at liberty to draw on our account for as much money as you require, for as long a period as you need it. We cannot bear to think of a work such as yours suffering through lack of funds. We desire the work of propogating the Word of God to go on, and we would like to help.

I wrote back telling them that we could not avail ourselves of their generous offer, as it was one of our principles never to run into debt, but that we were deeply grateful to them. By return of post came a substantial money order, followed by another each month. God's work done in God's way can never lack God's supplies.

So in varying ways the needs were supplied. A commercial traveller happened to pass through our village, saw our need of medical supplies, and sent us a large consignment of all the products that his firm still had in stock—the last we were to have for years. When the Jewish doctor was compelled by the authorities to relinquish his practice, he handed us all his remaining medicines. Kabyles would call in with a gift of oil or figs. European farmers supplied us with wheat to be ground and made into unleavened bread—baked in a frying pan! Someone dropped a fleece of wool into our garden so that it could be washed, spun into knitting wool, and used to knit the clothes which we so desperately needed during the snowy weather. Apricot trees and vines, which had never born fruit before, yielded bumper crops, enabling us to dry the fruit for use in winter. The walnut tree produced ten times more than ever before. Ash leaves mixed with dried branble leaves made excellent tea! In so many small ways God provided. The situation was really acute when baby was born. We had literally come to the end of all supplies. The next morning there was a sharp knock at the front door. This was unusual so early in the morning, and baby's birth had meant a bad night. On opening the door no person could be seen, but sitting on the doorstep was a big hamper. In it was a large chicken, five pounds of butter, four or five cream cheeses, ten pounds of sugar, twelve pounds of white flour and—some coffee! We had not had any of these things for months. Last, but not least, were some old sheets to be used to make nappies for the baby. We wept for joy and said, 'Thank you, God.'

After the fall of France the Axis troops invaded Tunisia and hundreds of refugees fled to eastern Algeria. Later the whole country passed under the control of German and Italian commissions. Our enemies seized on this opportunity to bring the spiritual work to a close. I was warned that all my movements were being closely watched by the Sureté, the French Secret Police. Many of the French people were deeply affected by the fall of France, and a series of weekly gatherings was organised to study the New Testament with a view to presenting the comfort and hope of the gospel. The French judge, the doctor, two sub-Administrators, the wives of the local police force, as well as many Jews, Protestants and Catholics were attending.

A well-conceived letter was sent to the headquarters of the Vichy French, in which we were accused of political propoganda in favour of General de Gaulle, who was at that time in England leading the Free-French. A list of all the people attending our meetings was attached to the letter. Quite suddenly a substantial police force appeared at Lafayette. A detailed investigation was made in every house except ours. Our friends were deeply concerned for our safety, and offered to take our son if we were eventually interned. They advised us to stop all spiritual work. What could I do under these circumstances? I went to see the local Administrator.

'Sir, I wish you to be quite frank with me, and to inform me of the accusations that have been brought against us.'

'I will be perfectly frank with you,' he replied. 'I can tell you nothing. However, you are quite free to continue your visits to the villages for preaching. If you have an agreement with the doctor to care for the sick at your outstation, then carry on. You are at liberty to continue all your classes and meetings; and your wife can visit the homes. But there must be no political activity.'

How incredible! With feelings running so high, cut off from all supplies from the homeland, threatened with internment, surrounded by powerful political and religious antagonists and without legal aid, the Administrator, a man of integrity and courage, had told us to continue every branch of God's work. The sequel is also almost incredible. All the leading men of the town were removed from their posts, the doctor lost his right to practice, the Administrator lost his place; his deputies were sent away; but the isolated servants of God, with absolutely no human aid, stayed on to continue God's work! Eventually all private cars, except those adjusted to run on methylated spirit, were off the road, but our car was still running with an 'SP' label, signifying *Services Publiques*. We were some of the very few to receive a modest ration of petrol each month until supplies were exhausted.

Practically all missionary work in Algeria was stopped, some missionaries were interned, many were living in towns under *residence surveillée,* and were unable to move among the people. Living conditions became increasingly difficult, buses ran with a huge boiler at the back which was stoked with wood or charcoal. Permission to travel even short distances had to be obtained from the police. Yet it was at this time that a small church was formed, and until we left for the UK in 1943 we continued our ministry, never at any time having less than fourteen classes and meetings each week.

The only way to reach the Hammam was to walk or to cycle. I was able to buy a very old decrepit cycle. The downhill journey to the Baths was delightful, even when carrying a rucksack full of stock medicines; but the long slog uphill in the noontide sun was very tiring. Medical supplies were eked out with herbal remedies which we prepared ourselves. Thousands still attneded the clinics and heard the Word of life. Numbers grew in the children's classes until over one hundred and twenty children were attending the five weekly classes for religious instruction. We purchased fleeces of wool and gave it to women to wash and spin into yarn; the class girls learned to knit and made many useful garments for themselves and families. There was a large class for small Arab girls. It was delightful to see them singing action choruses and holding their little hands out as Pearl taught them to pray in Jesus' name. In the street they would run up so trustfully and catching hold of her hands, one on each side, would lead her to their homes where she was able to share the comfort of the Scriptures with their mothers in those very hard times. Europeans dare not show friendship, but the trustful love of the Muslim children was a great cheer during those years when we were ostracised and despised because of our nationality. Forty homes were open to Pearl, and all wanted the gospel. It was impossible at that time to buy any material in the shops, but she spent most of her spare time in making garments for babies and children from old clothes. Many died through cold and exposure. Some families had only one ragged garment for the whole family. They would stay in bed under the one wretched blanket, and take it in turn to get a little exercise, wearing the one garment. Some made a rough shirt out of a sack with holes for the arms.

The little church grew. Basheer was baptised at the same time as Kakoo. Zeetoonee was too weak to be baptised, but never missed a meeting. Tayeb and others came up from the Hammam each Sunday morning. What a joy it was to hear worship and praise ascending to the Lord from these erstwhile Muslim lips. It was worth the isolation, the sacrifice, the loneliness, even though bitter persecution eventually brought the church to nothing. Basheer was poisoned, Zeetoonee died, Ali was poisoned and after many years Kakoo turned to witchcraft. The heartbreak of Muslim work.

With what amazement we listened to the announcement over the radio in September 1942 telling that British and American troops had landed in Algeria. Throughout those long dark years of war, when there were no papers from England, each evening we had carefully locked the outside gate, placed heavy blankets over the windows, and had tuned in to London, turning the set down to a mere whisper, and listening to the news. Long convoys of troops were soon travelling on the main roads. I felt that I must see them for myself, so, mounting the decrepit old cycle I rode twenty-five miles to the main road. The military must have thought that I was mad, as I stood by the roadside cheering. They never imagined that I was English, and of course the convoy could not halt. It was not long before we had some of them in our home, and went along to the camps for services.

At the end of June, Pearl and I and the two children embarked at Algiers on a former Dutch liner for the United Kingdom. The usual four-day journey took well over a month. We were attacked by German planes shortly after we left Gibralter. We chased German submarines. The two cruisers and the four destroyers did a good job, and we arrived safely on Merseyside. How thankful we were for the protecting hand of God during that voyage in war time with two children. In England people were complaining of short rations; but to be able to eat butter and cheese, margarine and jam once again was wonderful. To have clothing coupons that we could use seemed too good to be true. Our hearts were still in Africa, and at the end of four months we were fully prepared to go back. We knew our God. We could trust him anywhere.

Chapter Eight

Ali

Once again we were faced with a difficult choice. On Armistice Day in May 1945 very serious riots broke out at Setif, and these extended to Lafayette and Lesser Kabylia. Over one hundred Europeans were cruelly massacred by the Muslims, and the French army retaliated by murdering thousands of nationals. It created an atmosphere of bitterness and hatred that was not conducive to mission work. Only the timely intervention of a French army officer had saved the whole European population of Lafayette from being massacred. The authorities refused to allow Pearl to return with me to Algeria. Again I had to choose between remaining in England with my wife and children, or returning alone to the work to which God had called me, and from which I had been unavoidably absent for just over a year. I returned alone, to a land of famine.

In spite of the disturbances the authorities allowed me to resume work in the villages. Petrol was available and the car was soon on the road. In the village of Zakoo a number of men and boys had gathered and were listening well to the story of the prodigal son. Suddenly the village sheikh appeared. He was a red-bearded gentleman with a very violent temper. Striking right and left with his thick stick, he scattered the boys and told the men to leave. Having dispersed my audience he retired to the mosque to pray! The men and boys came back to listen, and the sheikh returned to the fray with renewed zeal. His heavy cudgel fell with sickening thuds on the backs of the boys. They all turned and fled before his fury. Snatching the chart depicting the broad and narrow ways, he flung it to the winds, and did the same with the New Testament from which I was teaching. Raising his thick stick over my head he cursed me, calling me a 'Christian dog', and demanded why I had dared to return to his village when he had told me to keep away. It was useless to try and continue under such circumstances, and I had no alternative but to leave. I did so with a heavy heart, and with the curses and threats of the sheikh ringing in my ears. The village chief followed me to the outskirts of the village and said, 'He has an awful temper, but in three months his term of office will be finished. We shall sack him and send him back to his village. After that you can return to us whenever you like.'

The following year I remembered the invitation to return, and I had a most encouraging time in the tribe. Towards evening, when I was wending my way over the mountains back to the car, after a long and tiring day, I heard a voice shouting to me, 'Oh sheikh, stop! Wait for me!' I had started the day at four in the morning and had been tramping over the mountains for twelve hours. I had spoken to groups of men in five villages, and was both mentally and physically tired out. Looking over my shoulder, I spotted a religious teacher hastening to overtake me. I at once recognised him as the brother of the red-bearded gentleman with the violent temper, the man who had so persistently opposed me the previous year. I hurried on. I was too tired to start another discussion, and was anxious to get home. The Muslim was so determined to overtake me that he actually condescended to run. 'Stop! Stop!' he shouted. He soon caught up with me. 'Why is it that you visit every other village in Kabylia, but you never come to us?' were his opening words. 'You never come to us, and there are men in our village who need your message, they really want to know.' I replied, 'On two occasions I have visted your hamlet, but not a single man has troubled to come and listen. You must also remember that some of your own family do not want me to preach the gospel. They are afraid that if Kabyles follow the Lord Jesus, they will no longer need you Muslim teachers. I myself have very strong proof that some of your own family are opposed.' 'Come to our village as soon as you can,' was the earnest request. 'Some people there really need you.'

At the earliest opportunity, but with considerable misgivings, I climbed up to the village from the road, and went to the quarter where the Marabouts, the religious leaders lived. There was no sign of my friend, or of his brother who had left the previous week to live in a distant town. I therefore went to the other quarter of the village where the Kabyles lived. A number had seen me coming and had gathered. They were seated on a large rock waiting for me. They welcomed me very cordially and encouraged me to speak to them. I had not proceeded very far when I was interrupted by Ali.

'Tell me, teacher, what must I do to have forgiveness for my sins?'

The Holy Spirit was at work. I outlined very simply the work of the Lord Jesus. 'Without the shedding of blood there is no forgiveness.' Jesus said, 'This is my blood of the covenant which is poured out for many for the forgiveness of sins.' 'Everyone who believes in him receives forgiveness of sins through his name.' Ali repeated the words from the Bible as they were read.

'Can I have forgiveness now?'

'Yes, if you will believe in the Lord Jesus.'

When the meeting was over, Ali followed me to the outskirts of the village. He said, 'Tell me again what I must do. Do you mean that I must simply repent and turn from all my efforts to find salvation and simply trust in the Lord Jesus?'

Ali trusted the Saviour that day. There was no doubt at all about his transparent sincerity and deep love for the Lord. Every fortnight I visited him in his village. Ali went from strength to strength and with my help taught himself to read, and studied the Bible. Through his faithful witness five or six others trusted the Saviour. It was the first time that a group of Christians was gathered in a Kabyle village. A very simple local church. What was interesting was that half a mile away there were the ruins of a Christian church, with a large baptistry which had been used for baptism by immersion. Nearly fifteen centuries before Christians had gathered there to worship God. The Lord had led me to that isolated village, the place which I had so studiously avoided. God used a most unusual means, making the wrath of man to praise him, showing clearly that he is Lord of all. Whatever efforts independent Algeria makes to prevent those groups from forming, the Omnipotent God will ultimately gather all those other sheep until there is one flock, one Shepherd. It was very evident that I must visit that village as often as possible.

Ali sat up on his bed and coughed. He was suffering from chronic TB of the lungs. During the war he had been trapped in Belgium, evacuated from Dunkirk to England, then sent back to France and eventually re-patriated. He had been nursed by a Roman Catholic sister who had spoken to him about the Lord Jesus and his atoning death; but there was so much that he could not understand until, by the leading of the Holy Spirit, I had visited his village and he had trusted the Saviour. Again he was seized with a violent fit of coughing. It was only with great effort that he was able to express his gratitude. He said, 'Thank God you came and told me about him before I die! We did not know that the glory of the Lord Jesus far outweighs that of Mohammed. No one ever told us that Jesus loved us and died for us. We did not know that God forgives all our sins when we trust the Lord Jesus. We thought that we could only hope for forgiveness after years of fasting and prayers. Thank God you came and told me about him before I die!'

It had been quite an effort for me to visit him that day. The snow which was melting on the surrounding mountains had swollen the stream in the ravine until it was an angry swirling torrent. I had seen the black clouds and the threatening storm before leaving the shelter of the car. I had been sorely tempted to continue my way home without attempting to visit that lonely child of God. It had been useless to attempt to cross the torrent at the usual ford. I went upstream for a mile, the snow turned to sleet and teeming rain until I found a convenient place to cross. Then I plunged knee deep into the icy water, and climbed up to a height of 3,000 feet. The rain again turned to snow, and gasping for breath, I fought my way through the blinding snow storm to arrive at last at the house of my friend and brother in Christ. It was good to sit in the smoke of the house, sipping a cup of black coffee, and munching a few figs with some dry unleavened bread. Ali's wife was no cook, but I had to make an attempt at enjoying the coffee, which tasted of paraffin. I was chilled to the bone, but how heart-warming to hear those words of the sick man, 'Thank God you came and told me before I die!'

Ali had a pension from the French army and a liberal allowance for his wife and children, so that he was independent. Most Muslim men of his age are dependent on their family. They share everything with their family, even with adult brothers, and are often unable to break away from Islam because of family ties. Ali was free to follow the Lord. Having heard the gospel and believed, he was determined to be a true disciple. Using the Laubach method he had taught himself to read in Kabyle. 'Each one teach one', was the motto, so that he was anxious to pay his debt and teach someone else to read. He soon found several apt pupils. All went well until one day he was asked,

'Ali, if we learn to read in Kabyle, what can we read?'

'The New Testament in Kabyle, of course,' he replied.

'But surely there are other books?'

'I will ask sheikh Abd alMasih,' he said.

'Can I read the newspaper in Kabyle?' asked one of his friends.

'No, but there is God's Word, and that is better than any newspaper.'

'Then we are to understand that you want us to read the New Testament and to become Christians. Perhaps you, too, are a Christian?'

'Yes, I believe that the Lord Jesus died for me,' replied Ali.

The reading lesson had ended in uproar. They had turned on Ali with bitter words, cursing him, spitting at him and telling him that he knew nothing. They brought along the village sheikh who did all in his power to overthrow the faith of this determined man. It was useless. Ali knew that his sins were forgiven. The news spread. From far and near men came to talk with him, and to find what was the reason for his joy and assurance. One learned man brought his Koran with him. After some hours of discussion with Ali, he pointed to the Koran and stated, 'There is no forgiveness in this book. I have read it from cover to cover, and it really has no message for me.' Then he listened avidly as Ali told him of the Son of man who has authority on earth to forgive sins.

The Muslim *ulama* (doctors) were deeply concerned. They felt compelled to stop this determined witness to Christ. He must either be brought back to the fold of Islam or be killed, but how? Ali had to report at hospital every three years for a check up. Failure to report at the appointed time would result in the loss of his pension. Here then was the way to force this despised Christian to return to Islam or to break him; to intimidate him or kill him. The village postman destroyed the first letter which fixed the date of the hospital appointment, then the second and finally the third. Meanwhile Ali waited for the letter which never came. At last he decided to take the long journey from his home in the mountains to Constantine, by donkey, bus and train.

The advice offered at the hospital was, 'Go back to your home and wait. We will inform you as soon as a bed in the hospital is available. Then you must return here at once.'

Ali returned to his mountain village, but no letter from the hospital ever reached him. The Muslims made quite sure that it never should. He lost his pension. He was penniless and needed medicines; wood to heat his home during the bitter days when snow lay all round, food for himself and family. He very reluctantly accepted a gift of five pounds from us, but he would take no more. His courage was undaunted. Every evening he gathered his family for prayer. He read to them from the New Testament. Peacock, his wife, professed conversion, his lovely young daughter also trusted the Saviour, and his elder brother did so too. It was evident that God was working. Ali himself was frightfully keen. He said to me, 'Sheikh, can you not arrange a special effort to tell the whole village about our Lord? Bring over a projector and a film strip. That will help the men to understand.' I disconnected the car battery, loaded it on to a donkey with the projector and screen, and we climbed up the narrow track to his village. There the screen was set up on a big rock, and the men gathered as soon as darkness fell. Now even the youngest, prettiest woman who was shut away, could creep out, and under cover of darkness, peep over the walls at the pictures. 'To seek and to save' was the title, and they all understood so well that three-fold parable of Luke 15 as I read it to them in their own language and explained it. How thrilled Ali was to be able to openly witness to his Lord in his own village. His brother's wife, a little hunchback, and his nephew professed to believe. There was now a group of Christians in this Kabyle village. They were so sincere, but fearful of the consequences of open confession of their faith. 'They would burn the house down over our heads if ever we came right out for the Lord and were baptised,' said his brother.

Meanwhile I had intervened with the French authorities, and after many months Ali was interviewed at the hospital, and the pension papers were renewed. Ali at once paid me back the meagre gift of five pounds that he had accepted in his deep distress. He insisted that he could not possibly accept the money from a servant of God when he had a pension. It was rather he who should give to God's work. He certainly was not a 'Rice Christian'. Our hearts were warmed. This is what we had worked and prayed for. An indigenous church in the centre of Kabylia, so near to the ruins of the building, where centuries earlier, Christians had worshipped Jesus Christ. Praise the Lord! How great is our God!

The strain of the past months had told severely on Ali. He realised to the full the cost of discipleship. 'If any man follow me, let him take up his cross.' The persistent opposition from his own people was extremely hard for a sick man to take. The insults from his neighbours, the spitting and cursing, the blatant refusal to help repair the roof when it leaked, were all like gall to this peace-loving man. He did rejoice that God had answered his prayer, and that his pension had been renewed so that he could pay all his debts. He himself felt too weak to undertake the ten-mile journey over the bleak mountains to withdraw his quarterly pension from the Post Office. I felt sure that this was where I could be of very real help. I offered to obtain a power of attorney, and take the money to him each quarter. However the whole Muslim population was determined to unite in opposition till the end. 'A foreigner has no right to set his foot in this Post Office,' the local post-master declared. They were Muslims and had to be heavily bribed before they would cash a money order for anyone, even a fellow Muslim. They knew that I would not give a bribe. At any price the pension papers must be kept in their hands. Only in this way could they succeed in utterly breaking the apostate from Islam.

Then the bitter blow fell. Ali had entrusted his pension papers to his nephew, and had instructed him to withdraw the money from the local Post Office. The nephew did not return to Ali that day. Many days passed and then he sent a message, 'I am so sorry. On the way back from the Post Office the mule wandered into the forest, and somehow the pension papers fell out of my pocket. Not only did I lose the papers, but all the money went too.' Ali was again a pauper; money, papers, everything was lost, and it meant months and months of endless formalities before the pension could be obtained. As he lay day after day in that bleak Kabyle hut and reflected on his lot, he lost his joy. He realised that he was at the mercy of these cruel relent-less Muslims. Why had God not intervened to stop them? Now some of his own family turned against him as no more money was forthcoming. Drugs were placed in his food and his mind was affected. Deep depression set in. Unable to work, surrounded by enemies, stric-ken with tuberculosis of the lungs, yet still loving the Lord, he sunk into the depths of despair. In vain I tried to persuade him to come to town where he could obtain efficient care and treatment, but he was ada-mant. He preferred to die in his own home.

There was only one thing for me to do. I could still continue to visit him in his village, to take him small delicacies, to read, comfort him, and pray with him. Then one day I arrived to find the door bolted and barred. Such a thing was unheard of in a Kabyle house during the day time. 'Ali, open the door and let me in,'

I called. There was no answer. Again I knocked and appealed to him, but there was dead silence. I knew he was there, stretched out on his rough bed. A neighbour shouted, 'Ali, it is your friend, the Christian who has come to see you.' Back from the sick man came the soul-chilling reply, 'Tell him to go away. I have not a friend in the world.' Never shall I forget the pathos of those words, the pang of sorrow that gripped my heart as, struggling to stifle the sobs and keep back the tears, I turned away and left the village. My only comfort was that I knew that in every pang that rends the heart the Man of sorrows has a part.

Ali died a few days later, and they buried him as a Muslim in a Muslim grave, even though he had steadfastly refused to witness to Mohammed and had died as a Christian. Even his enemies were compelled to admit that. His poor body lies in a Muslim cemetery just outside his village, one of the many who at the coming of the Lord Jesus will rise from Muslim cemeteries to meet the Lord in the air: 'He shall see the fruit of the travail of his soul and be satisfied.' Surely that one soul was worth all the effort, the travail, the sorrow and the pain; yet pain mingled with joy to see the evidence of new life in a Muslim through the working of the Spirit of God.

Come tell me all that you have said and done,
    Your victories and failures, hopes and fears,
I know how hardly souls are wooed and won,
    My choicest wreaths are always wet with tears.

Chapter Nine

A Strategic Centre

How wonderful it was, after a year's absence, to welcome Pearl and baby Ruth back to Lafayette and home! Once more she was able to resume the visits to the women and take up the girls classes.

It became increasingly evident that, whilst the major part of the population was being evangelised through the clinics and visits to the villages, some means must be found to contact enquirers. An interested man could not be expected to make a journey of fifty miles to find out more about Christianity. A centre in Kabylia was most desirable. It was obvious that the best place would be near the big weekly market at Beni Ourtilane. Every Friday between five and ten thousand men would attend the market, according to the time of year. The difficulty would be to obtain a site for the erection of a building. To rent a room would be to court disaster, for as soon as numbers of people began to attend, the owner would give us notice to quit.

In Kabylia the Old Testament law of redemption still holds good. Every effort is made to retain property or ground in the family, or at least in the hands of Kabyles. If a stranger purchases land, any member of the family can step in and reclaim the land, paying back the purchase money. For this reason, for many years no missionary had been able to purchase ground in the mountains. The whole population was opposed to sell-ing to a European. I finally succeeded in finding a man who had no near kinsman with the right to redeem. From him we purchased a large piece of ground on the outskirts of the market, near a fountain, and which was situated between two roads. In that tribe there were thirty villages, and many others in the neighbouring tribes.

As soon as possible after the Second World War, we quarried the stone, I hired a stone mason and the building started. On the very first day a man approached us. 'What are you doing here? Building a Christian mosque? Not a single person will come near you. We shall not allow them. May God curse the religion of your forefathers.' It was a clear warning of the coming storm of opposition. I replied that we would finally win through and overcome their bitter hatred. 'How will you ever do that?' 'We shall do it by love.'—A hall seating forty five people, a small room with two bunk beds and a garage were erected. Then the hall was furnished. The market place was surrounded by about forty buildings, coffee houses, a baker's shop, several grocers, and administrative offices. Later a large police station, schools and dispensary were erected.

An eastern market is always an attraction. Huge piles of oranges, cabbages, water melons, potatoes, tomatoes and peppers, tempt the prospective buyer. In the summer there are heaps of grapes, peaches, pomegranates, melons and prickly pears. The purchaser is allowed to turn over the fruit and pick out the best, rejecting any that is blemished or substandard. In another section of the market, each man has small leather sacks made from goat skins and containing lentils, beans or chick-peas. There are huge piles of wheat and barley. When measuring the cereals, the bushel is filled and the corn piled up to form a cone. If the buyer can add another grain, he is at liberty to do so! Figs are lightly pressed into the measure. Oil is poured in until it runs over. The whole market area is filled with a motley throng of men. Not a woman or girl can be seen. Just outside the market some very old women sit with a few eggs for sale. The Arab doctor spreads his wares on a lion's skin. He sells anything from bitter aloes to antimony to beautify the eyes. (Eye shadow was used in Algeria long before it came into fashion in England.) The dentist demonstrates his ability to extract any tooth with his finger and thumb, without drawing blood! A pile of teeth nearly a foot high testifies to his success. Droves of sheep, herds of cattle, and some goats are crowded together in the animal section.

Every Friday morning, I left home soon after five o'clock and travelled by car to Beni Ourtilane. There were plenty of chores to do when I arrived. They included lighting a fire, preparing a midday meal, sweeping and dusting the hall. It was not long before the first boys arrived. Flannelgraph, film strips, Bible stories all proved an attraction. Each Friday about sixty boys would come, and this meant having a series of talks with them before they went up to the Market. Then men would start to come down from the market, asking for advice or desiring to talk over spiritual things. Round about half-past ten, I would go up to the market, walk round and chat with men that I knew, and purchase fruit and vegetables. Then back to the Hall. Any interested men now knew that I was available for reading the Word of God. Lakhdar, Yousef, Tehar, Ali and others trusted the Saviour at that Hall in the mountains.

At about one o'clock in the afternoon, the men would start leaving the market to return to their villages. No work would be done on market day, so I visited the surrounding villages in turn, returning to my room to pass the night. Then early on Saturday morning the sick people would start arriving. I worked on until midday or after, preaching, caring for the sick, extracting teeth, opening abscesses and performing minor operations, as has already been described for the

Hammam outstation. Pearl accompanied me as often as possible. She would go to the women in the nearby villages, in the afternoon we would go out together, Pearl in the houses and myself with the men. Then we would pass Saturday night at Beni Ourtilane, sleeping in the bunk beds placed one over the other. In this way there was an ever widening outreach, and we can honestly say that from fifty to sixty per cent of the population of the whole area heard the message of salvation.

Aith Moussa is a large village situated in the mountains about 4,000 feet above sea level. Every two months I visited this group of villages, leaving Beni Ourtilane as soon as the market started to empty, travelling with the men to their village, chatting in the coffee houses, spending the night in a Kabyle house, and returning to base very early the following morning to prepare for the patients. On one of these visits I heard a voice calling me, 'Ai sheikh, come over here. We badly need you!' The two oxen had been fighting and the eye of one had been gouged out. They wanted me to treat the suppurating wound! Then I was taken to see a little girl in the throes of fever, an old lady with a racking cough, and finally a shut-in woman suffering from chronic opthalmia. I noted the names of each one in my book, told the man to bring some bottles to the clinic next day, and went on to the coffee house. It was full of men playing dominoes and cards. They were seated on mats round low tables, smoking and talking loudly. The atmosphere was that of a bar. I took off my shoes and left them with those of the men outside the door, found my way across the mats, dodging between the men and the tables, and found a position where I could control the whole audience with my eyes. Then I sat down.

'What will you have, skeikh, coffee or tea?'

'Coffee, please.'

'How would you like it? Sweet, bitter-sweet, strong

or just right?'

'Give me a *gedged*, please.' A *gedged* is just right, not too sweet, not too bitter, but almost thick enough for the small coffee spoon in it to stand up alone! I sipped the coffee while I waited. The men at the next table had finished their game. Then another group finished, I was conscious that all the men were now silent and watching me intently. Then one man who was wrapped round in his long woollen burnous spoke up, 'Now, sheikh, we're waiting for you. Get out the Book and read to us again.' There was no need for him to tell me which Book, I only carried one. Amid murmurs of approval they listened to the message. Half an hour passed. My message that day was hard-hitting, practical and personal; aimed at leading each individual to trust the living Saviour who had died for his sins, even the sins of these Kabyle men. Having finished the message, I prepared to leave. 'How much is the coffee?'

'That is paid for, sheikh. We Kabyles do not let our teachers pay for their coffee. Don't be too long before you return.' I went on to the next village, reflecting on the deep soul thirst in Muslim hearts.

The sun was sinking in a ball of fire beneath the horizon. The voice of the muezzin calling the faithful to prayer rang out. That was always the signal for me to bring my message to a close. I distributed booklets to those who could read, and waited until prayers were finished. I was quite sure that in a few minutes someone would offer me shelter for the night and an evening meal. Prayers over, the men left the mosque, walked past me without a word, and each one went to his home. A fresh cold wind blew down from the mountain which overshadowed the village. The shepherd boys came in with their sheep and goats, whistling, prodding, urging them on. A man with a couple of bullocks moved by, carrying on his shoulders the heavy wooden plough. He entered his house, passing through the massive

wooden doors of the courtyard immediately facing me.
Shortly afterwards they closed with a thud and the
heavy wooden bolts were slipped into place. Then all
was silent. Darkness fell. One by one I heard the head
of each house shut the door, securing it with the
massive bars. No one would go out until morning. At
the break of day each man would reopen the door and
it would stay open all day. Inside the houses the sleeping mats had been spread on the ground, and the
women would soon be laying out the bedding and the
whole family would retire for the night. The scene was
so familiar to me. So often had I shared their fire, par-
taken of their meal, and enjoyed their fellowship. But
tonight I was shut out. I waited on, chilled to the
marrow. Once more the call of the sheikh rang out
through the pitch black night. It was *Laasha*, the last
prayer of the day, just one hour after sunset. From
some homes came the low murmur of voices as the
family drew closer to the warmth of the fire, and dis-
cussed the events of the day. It was really cold in these
mountains when the sun had set. I sat and shivered in
the icy mountain air.

There was no doubt in my mind now. This was a
studied insult, planned hostility. The laws of Kabyle
hospitality had been ignored, the guest left outside in
the cold. I realised now that I must find my way back
over those bleak cold mountains. I set out to walk
through the sleeping village. Even the dogs were silent,
for which I was profoundly thankful. A pack of dogs on
a dark night can be quite dangerous. It really was dark,
pitch black. I walked through the cemetry, past the
graves, climbing up the rough pathway strewn with
stones and boulders. Now and again I stumbled and
nearly fell. What was that? It was only the screech of an
owl as it flew near my head. Close by a jackal howled,
and it was answered by several others just below the
road. I was hungry, utterly weary and chilled to the
bone by the icy wind. Up and up I climbed until I

reached the place where the path narrowed to a couple of feet. Below was a sheer drop of two hundred meters. My nailed boots slipped on the polished surface of the rock. I pulled myself together. It would not do to get the jitters now! Again the ominous hoot of a night bird pierced the air. No Kabyle man would have taken such a journey at night over those mountains alone. Yet—I was not alone! 'I will never leave you nor forsake you.' The verse rang continuously in my mind. What sweet assurance from my ever-present Lord! Yet, humanly speaking, I felt terribly alone. I thought of the time in the life of the Lord Jesus when, 'They went each to his own house, but Jesus went to the Mount of Olives.' I felt utterly spent, totally fagged out at the end of a long busy day spent for others. I sat down on a rock and looked down to the villages. Here and there a light still flickered. The sounds of village life still came up, a few men were still moving round down there. But I was turned out, rejected, hated, because I was a Christian, unwanted by the very people I was trying so hard to help. I prayed for them—and then unashamedly wept.

I finally reached my room in the early hours of the morning, and threw myself on the bed; utterly weary and sad at heart, discouraged because of the hardness of the way. Why does God in his infinite wisdom permit such heart-breaks? Surely it is to bring his servants into closer fellowship with himself, to allow them to enter more fully into the fellowship of his sufferings. Viewed in that way, what a tremendous privilege it is!

There is however a sequel to this story. The following morning I was awakened from sleep and called from bed quite early.

'*Sebah alkheyr, ya sheikh* (Good morning, sheikh). Hurry up and open the door. I have brought the bottles. Give me my medicine at once, and let me get back to work.' It was one of the men from that village to which I had gone the previous day.

The hall filled up and I started to give the message.

The Kabyle mind is always alert and quick to grasp the meaning of a parable, and I decided to tell of my experience the night before. I began,

'This morning I have a story to tell you all. Yesterday I met a man in a village not too far from here who greatly values my skill and my medicines. He is here today. Last night I sat outside his door. He saw me, and knew well that I needed shelter and warmth, but he left me sitting in the street, outside his house, at his door. He really wanted my medicines and my care. He ardently desired all I had to give him, but he did not want *me*. This morning he has come to the door of my house, and he expects me to receive him and give him anything that he asks for. Now may I read to you all from the Word of God? The Lord Jesus says, "Behold, I stand at the door and knock; if any one hears my voice and opens the door, I will come in to him and eat with him, and he with me!" Today the Lord Jesus stands at your heart's door. You know that he wants to come in. You want his gifts of forgiveness and eternal life, of peace with God. You like to listen to his Word, but you leave him outside. You do not want him. You reject him. Listen again. The same Lord Jesus says in his Word, "When once the householder has risen up and shut the door, you will begin to knock at the door saying, 'Lord, Lord, open to us.' He will answer you, 'I do not know where you come from.'"—Luke 13:25-27. Those are his words to you now. Tormorrow you will be standing at his door. What will he say to you then, if today you have refused to admit him into your heart? Now go back to your village and take this message with you and tell it to all.'

The following market day several leading men of that village called to express their regret at the incident, asking me to return and to spend the night in their house. I did so the next week, for love is not resentful, love bears all things, believes all things, hopes all things, endures all things. But it had hurt to be left out in the cold, and the more so because I loved them.

Beni Ourtilane eventually served as a base for the further extension of the work. A rough motor road led past the hall and on through the tribe to a group of five villages. I often visited this tribe. Some of the men asked if it would be possible to have a series of meetings with them in their village. An old disused coffee house was made available, rent free. I set up my camp bed in half of the building, and spread some rush mats in the other section. Each morning I devoted to the care of sick people; the afternoons were spent with the men, and when the boys came out of school I held a class for them. Then, after the evening meal, men from the five villages gathered for a men's meeting.

To live alone among the people for a fortnight was quite a new experience. Darkness fell, the sheikh had called to prayer. The room of the coffee house was ready, lit by the burner of an acetylene lamp. I had very carefully prepared the message that night, for I was to speak on the Deity of Christ. It is the foundation truth of the gospel, but a most difficult subject to take up with Muslims. I was responsible to God for those men. It meant that I must not only speak the truth, but somehow communicate the wonderful fact that Jesus Christ is God incarnate. 'What do you think of the Christ?' was the challenge. I spoke of his pre-existence, his virgin birth, his spotlessly pure life, his mighty power, his superlative titles, his atoning death, his glorious resurrection, his wonderful ascension, his present seat at God's right hand, and his glorious return. It was the first time that I had ever dared to deal with such a vast, yet all-important subject, with an audience of Muslims. How would they receive it? What would be their reaction to such a message? They were living in the security of their environment, anticipating a speedy victory in the war for Independence, which they were fully aware would soon begin. Then Islam would reign supreme and unchallenged throughout their land. I had very good cause to fear the outcome of such a talk at such a time. Yet I felt it must be given. I was entirely in their hands, sleeping as their guest in their tribe, in a loaned coffee house with no locks to the doors. I was very, very conscious of my own utter weakness; yet I had a very deep conviction that God had given me the message that night. The Holy Spirit gave me wonderful liberty, the meeting closed and the men filed out silently.

Several of them were lurking outside in the darkness. I could just discern their forms. They moved towards the coffee house. So this was it. 'Lord, help me to be faithful.' was my prayer. The first man approached. 'Sheikh, that was really wonderful. It is just what we all want to know.' He left and another man came in.

'Tell us more like that. Thank you for that wonderful message.' Yet another came 'May God bless you. Our teachers never tell us anything like that. It really did my heart good.'

Then came an offer not to be despised. 'I will place this large olive press, and the adjoining room at your disposal. You can have them rent-free for as long as you like to come to us. Try and come at least once a week.' My heart leaped for joy. These were the men who had so violently opposed the work when it started. Now they were providing the means for a weekly meeting!

So on Saturday afternoons I travelled down to that group of villages, holding an afternoon clinic, and a men's meeting in the evening. Then there was that long journey back to Lafayette, along the narrow dangerous roads skirted by steep precipices. How very worth while it is to win the confidence of Muslims! It can be done.

Chapter Ten

The Valley of the Shadow

The struggle for independence in Algeria commenced on November 1st 1954, when Europeans travelling in the Aures mountains were ambushed and, in Kabylia, stacks of cork were fired and police posts attacked. For some months the war was limited. Cars were held up, individuals were threatened that they would be killed if they did not obey the orders of the National Liberation Front. Many were mutilated by the removal of ears and noses, or were otherwise maimed. At the outset the whole movement was political, but it was fomented by the religious leaders who proclaimed it to be a 'holy war,' to drive the infidels from their land. During 1955, bands of insurgents armed with guns, knives and sub-machine guns roamed the whole country, but they were to be found chiefly in the mountainous regions of Kabylia and the Aures. The work at Lafayette and the three outstations continued during this period, and I felt that I must make a special effort to reach the villages, so that two hundred and fifty were evangelised that year.

I had been warned. The village was situated in a lonely part of the country amidst aleppo pines; surrounded by steep precipitous slopes of scree and shale. I was told, 'It would be far wiser to leave them alone, for last year they killed twelve men, simply murdered them in cold blood. They are paid assassins. For as little as five pounds they will undertake to kill a man by poisoning him, or by shooting him; but they normally charge fifty. They are dangerous and not to be trusted, so mind your step. You have been warned.'

Yes, I certainly listened, but should I as a servant of God, go to them in spite of the warning? They were men for whom Christ died. But how should I approach them? With some trepidation I went into that village and chatted with the men. Then I opened my New Testament and read from the Galatian epistle, 'The fruit of the Spirit is love, joy, peace, longsuffering, gentleness, goodness, faith, meekness, temperance, against such there is no law. Now the works of the flesh are adultery...hatred, variance...envyings, murders.' I paused.

'Is it possible that there are murderers in this village?' I asked.

'There are at least forty. Nearly every man in this village has taken life,' was the solemn reply. They listened quietly to the Word of God, but the silence was ominous. I left the village and went back to the car which I had left by the roadside.

Below the road was another very large village. Should I go down to the men there? I had visited the village ten years previously in the company of a fellow worker, and we had been driven out, sent off with abusive words. Now I was alone. I turned aside into the forest to pray. I still remember the battle that went on in my mind. I could see the men in the village below me as they went in and out of the mosque, looking as small as ants. My heart almost failed me for fear. How could I go alone? Yet it was my duty to go, a solemn debt to God. I took out my English New Testament. One word stood out clearly, 'I can do all things through Christ who strengthens me.' Strengthened by this promise, but still anxious and fearful, I went down to face the bitter opposition. It did not come. Instead, eighty men gathered and listened intently as I told of a living Saviour. There were unseen listeners that day of whom I knew nothing.

Nearly a year later, in a village more than fifty miles away, a woman sat and listened to Pearl.

'Do you know, a man came into our village and told the men just what you are telling us women now? I listened to him, and that day I believed in the Lord Jesus.'

'That man is my husband,' said Pearl.

'Well, our men cannot forget the message that your husband gave them that day. For weeks they talked about it in their homes.'

How good is the God we serve! How very gracious of him to use his fearful hesitating servants.

The sun was setting as I wended my way back to the tent which had been pitched by the road-side. I was met by the Kabyle man whom I had left to guard the tent and to prepare the evening meal.

'*Laselama, ya sheikh* (Return in peace, teacher), there was no need for me to light the primus tonight. They have sent across couscous and meat from that other village.' (I was fully aware that the meal had been sent from the assassins' village.)

'Praise God for that, get out two plates and we will eat together.'

'No, sheikh; it is all for you. I have eaten my share already.'

I insisted that we eat together, as we had done every day, but my Kabyle man was adamant. 'OK, then you can pitch the stuff into the ravine,' I said. There was no doubt about it. That food was poisoned.

The next day I visited several villages, and Mohand, my Kabyle man, returned across the mountains to his home. I was to spend the last night of the tour alone, only a few miles away from the assassins' village. I chose a lonely spot where I was to camp for the night. It was four thousand feet above sea level, delightfully situated in a forest of fragrant pines. The slopes of the mountain fell away steeply to deep ravines where jackals lurked and wild boar roamed. There was just one house near by, and the Post Office. I knew that I could always obtain water there, and it was comforting to know that I should be near a Government employee. The situation throughout the country was very tense and feelings were running high. Already many on both sides had lost their lives in this struggle for independence. I parked the car near to the Post Office, and scrambled down the steep stony path to the mosque a mile below. A small company of men had already gathered there, and they seemed to hunger for the Word.

The sun was sinking below the horizon as I left the hamlet and climbed up the steep road back to the car. A fierce Arab dog persisted in following me. My past experience with these half-wild beasts had made me very wary, and as this shaggy dog continued to follow I felt most uneasy. So often I had been attacked by one of these fierce animals, never friendly to a stranger, which leap at one's throat. Standing with my back to a wall, I would swing my bag until someone came to call the dogs off. But here in the mountains there was no one to help. Picking up large stones, I aimed them at the dog time and again, but he persistently followed. I hastened my steps. Climbing up the steep mountain path, panting for breath, I finally reached the car. The dog still followed. I started up the car, drove to the forester's house, but not a soul could be seen. He and his family had been evacuated to a safer place. I then called at the Post Office to replenish my stock of water, but to my dismay, there was no one there either. I learned later that it was far too dangerous for any official to spend the night at such an isolated spot at such a time. The man slept with his family, surrounded by friends in the village below.

There was an uncanny feeling of stillness as I unlocked the car boot, got out the tent and pitched it, set up my camp bed and lit the primus. The dog was still there, prowling round at a distance, but getting closer. It looked like a huge grey wolf in the twilight. One more attempt to drive it off with stones seemed to succeed, and it slunk away into the night. I cooked a little macaroni for supper and then took one last look round at the car before turning in for the night. That wretched dog was still there, looking fierce and threatening. I made yet another effort to drive it away, pelting it with a volley of stones. Twilight faded, darkness fell. Not a single person was about. The road was deserted. It was uncanny.

I was dead tired, and I stretched out on the camp bed and fell sound asleep. At midnight I was awakened by a strange noise. Sitting up in bed I reached out for my torch and flashed it on. To my dismay I saw that the savage dog had crawled under the tent wall and was now fast asleep beside my bed! What was that? A twig cracked, someone was about. The dog growled. Again I switched on my pocket lamp and had a good look round. To my utter astonishment the bread and macaroni which had been left over from supper were on the plate under my bed untouched. I had been so tired that I had fallen asleep leaving the food under the bed. I rubbed my eyes. It seemed incredible. The food was still there, untouched by the savage, half-famished dog. I drew up the blanket, but sleep was impossible. At the break of dawn I was up. I called the dog outside, gave it the food which it quickly ate. A quick wash, followed by a cup of coffee, and I struck the tent, folding it and packing it in the boot of the car. I started the engine, and not till then did the dog turn away. My faithful friend, the dog which I had so cruelly stoned, trotted away down the mountain path, wagging his tail with evident pleasure, his task complete. Why did that dog follow so persistently one who treated it so badly? Why did it come? Who sent it? I am quite sure that the God who cared for Daniel, watched over me that night. Danger was near, my Lord knew and watched over me. I have proved him over so many years and in so many situations. The promise 'I am with you always' is no idle word. Just why God should send a dog on that occasion, I shall never know, but I know him enough to trust his wisdom, love and power.

That was the last tour I ever made to the more distant villages. The weekly visits to Beni Ourtilane continued, and each Friday afternoon I visited the surrounding villages systematically. A good number of men had gathered at Houria, and it was sunset before I left to climb up to our mountain home. It was a good hour's walk. Darkness quickly fell, and it was impossible to see more than a few feet ahead. Suddenly I heard the sound of muffled footsteps, and before I realised just what was happening, I was surrounded by a band of sturdy youths. A light shone on my face for an instant, and someone exclaimed,

'Why, it is sheikh!'

'Sheikh, are you not afraid to be out alone at night with all that is happening around?' they said.

'I am not alone.' In a moment they were on the alert and peered into the darkness. Suddenly they realised what I meant. I had an unseen Companion.

'No, sheikh, of course you are not alone. *Ror ek alhaq.* (You are right). Go in peace and may God protect you, and make your way easy.'

Another twenty minute's climb brought me to our lonely outpost and to bed.

The lonely night journey back from Karriouakli each Saturday was a tremendous challenge. Was I justified in risking my life to still reach those men? Was it wise to travel back home every Saturday night? Surely to do so was to court disaster, for it was the regularity which made it so dangerous. It would be so easy for the rebels to set a trap. 'Behold I have set before you an open door.' 'The night comes when no man can work.' These were the words of my Lord to me. I must go on.

At this time road blocks were frequent. Large stones or trees would be placed across the road, and this would compel the driver of a car or bus to stop. The next morning the blackened, burned-out hulk of the car, and the mutilated bodies of the occupants told their own sad tale. Outside the towns no one moved after dark. The nationals openly boasted, 'The country is ours after sunset. Then we control everything.'

It was nine o'clock at night. The men's meeting over, I was driving back to Lafayette, following the winding road from Kabylia. Quite suddenly, at a turning in the road, the car lights lit up the huge stones and boulders that completely blocked the road. The stones were much too large to allow the car to pass. There was an eerie stillness; not a soul could be seen. I quickly breathed a prayer, 'Lord, I am thine. The work is thine. Please get me through this.' Then I saw that by driving the car into the ditch I could just scrape through. 'Praise the Lord.' Another ten miles and I was nearly home. 'Halt, hands up.' A bright light shone in my eyes and completely dazzled me, the muzzle of a tommy-gun was pointed at my chest. *'Qui est-ce?* (Who is it?)' It was the local gendarmes who had stopped me. They were keeping a look-out on the road just below their headquarters. 'It is very unsafe to travel at night, Monsieur le Pasteur. Better wait until this little trouble is over. It will only go on for a few weeks. Then you can travel freely. But now—you know that after dark you are in their hands.' That is what they thought, but I knew that my life was in stronger, wiser, better hands.

So the work went on. By the end of the year over a hundred thousand security forces were in Algeria, but in spite of this the atrocities multiplied. Both sides were involved. Rival bands roamed the land. Plunder, rape, arson and murder were the order of the day. Personal grievances of long standing, tribal feuds, religious animosity and false accusations, were all made the excuse for widespread slaughter. But God's work went on.

I shall never forget my last visit to the little Hall in the mountains. I had spent Friday morning with men and boys from the market, and the afternoon in the villages. Saturday was a public holiday and I realised that few, if any, would come to the dispensary. I left the shelter of the outstation at four in the morning, just as dawn was breaking over those lovely mountains, the mountains where death lurked in every ravine and from every high crest. Driving along the forest road for eight miles, I noticed that the whole area was blackened by the burnt trees and bushes which had been destroyed so that they would not provide shelter for an ambush. I parked the car on the side of the road, in a deserted spoit, miles from any village or house, and committed it to the care of my Father, the One who had never failed. I shouldered my bag of tracts and books and started my long walk over the rough road. An hour's walk brought me to the first village. An old man asked, 'What happened last night? The powder spoke.' I assured him that I knew nothing. It transpired later that a band of men had held up the bus travelling down from the market at Beni Ourtilane. They had gone on to set fire to the bulldozer that was making a new road, had taken prisoner the four watchmen and had spent the night in the very group of villages in which I now found myself. I knew nothing of all this.

The men were in good humour. Thirty gathered in each of the first two villages. Not a word was said of any trouble, and they listened well to the message, and thanked me warmly for still going to them at such a time. I crossed the stream to the villages on the other side, and as I talked to the men of this hamlet, I heard someone calling from a distance. Not until then did I see that troops were deployed everywhere. Then the men told me all that had happened the preceding night.

The troops and the burned-out bulldozer were between me and the car. Other vehicles, both army and civilian, had been destroyed, but I found later that my car was intact, watched over by invisible eyes, in safe keeping indeed.

I ate my sandwiches and moved on to the last village. Exactly sixteen men gathered and sat on the stones of the public meeting place in the open air. Every detail of the scene stands out clearly in my mind until this day. The knoll rising steeply behind me, with the burned out bulldozer now clearly visible. Hundreds of troops all round with their machine guns and rifles at the ready. It was very obvious that as soon as I had completed my ministry I must face the music. What a solemn setting for a gospel meeting. I reminded my hearers that the wages of sin is death, of their need of forgiveness and of the One who had brought forgiveness, salvation and new life.

Meanwhile the troops were hurling great boulders down the mountain side into the ravine which bordered the village. Suddenly the rattle of a machine gun broke the stillness. Were they firing at us? No, it was simply an attempt to scare us. The bullets were directed into the ravine to my right. The immediate reaction in such circumstances is to take cover, but one of the Kabyles turned to his friends and said, 'Stay where you are, all of you. They are watching us closely.' Then, turning to me he said, 'Sheikh, carry on. Finish your message.'

That was the most difficult thing that I had to do, but with God's help, I went on to tell of salvation and a life which is eternal. It was the last message that I was ever to give in that village. I shook hands with them and said, 'Goodbye.' Then I went to face the authorities. I found the military gathered round the wreck of the bulldozer. The local gendarmes saw me and exclaimed, 'It is Monsieur le Pasteur. We thought it was a rebel leader.' I approached our local Administrator, who also was there, and expressed my regret at such wanton destruction. It was very obvious that the military authorities were distinctly annoyed with me. Appearances were all against me. It seemed as if I was hand-in-glove with the rebels. The next day two army captains called at our home. They interrogated me for two hours, asking questions about every aspect of our work and life. In the end one of them turned to me and said, 'How long have you been in this country?' 'Nearly forty years.' 'Well, if at the end of forty years our intelligence service has not found you out, either they are no good, or you are not working against us. But in future mind your step when you go to the villages.' I knew that if ever I did return, a stray French bullet might well endanger my life.

The following week the whole area surrounding Beni Ourtilane was evacuated by the French army, and a control post was established just below Lafayette. I realised that the people of those five hundred villages, which I had visited so regularly for so many years, had heard the Good News from me for the last time. The night had come, the night when no man can work.

From our home at Lafayette we watched the long convoy of various vehicles as it wound its way into Lafayette. It was composed of army lorries laden with equipment and furniture from the police station, schools and European's homes, and accompanied by tanks and armoured cars. The French army had evacuated Lesser Kabylia. The road to Beni Ourtilane was cut in over forty places by the rebel army, the bridges were blown up, and every European building in the area was completely destroyed. Every school, post office, forester's house and farm was burned to the ground by the rebels. The whole area where for more than thirty years I had gone about doing good and exercising a ministry of healing and preaching was now a battle field. The outstations in the mountains were in the hands of the Nationalists. They could no longer be used. We had been given no opportunity to bring out our furniture.

Many of the villages were pro-French and others had Nationalist sympathies. Whole villages were devastated; in some places, the whole population perished. A survivor from one village told me, 'They suddenly came on us and demanded food and shelter. To refuse meant death. They took the very best of everything. All our young men were taken as conscripts for the army. Our animals were driven away. We were compelled at the point of the sword to empty our store cupboards of figs corn and oil.'

The marauding bands were tracked down by aircraft, attacked with rockets, bombs and machine guns. The French systematically bombed the whole area, and later went in with troops. Years afterwards I sat and listened, heavy-hearted to a Frenchman who described how he had been in charge of a squad of men who had gone into a large village, and in cold blood massacred two hundred and sixty-two of our dear Kabyles. No mercy had been shown. Men, women, children, unborn babes all met the same fate. Then they had completely destroyed every house and gone on to repeat the operation in a second large village. They had met with no opposition. This man seemed to glory in the achievement, and admitted that his hand still itched to hold a gun and to feel his finger on the trigger. Such is war.

After five months the French army fought its way back to Beni Ourtilane. They found our Hall intact. God had preserved it through the fighting and the bombing. The Muslims had respected it as a house of God. They had heard the Word of God expounded there. It was there that they had prayed and seen the love of Christ in action. The building stood alone among the ruins, a silent testimony to the power of love. A Kabyle Christian was present when the army destroyed it. It was deliberately smashed to pieces, and everything it contained was rendered useless.

For many months I was denied permission to travel up to see the ruins, but eventually I was allowed to travel up in my own car, and joining a French army convoy. A sad sight met my eyes. All the doors and window frames had been removed and taken away to serve as fuel for the barracks. The dividing wall between the Hall and the bedroom had been broken down. The floor was one mass of Scripture portions, broken chairs, bottles of medicine, tiles, saucepans, broken crockery, twisted bedsteads, tins of ointment, and Bibles. So much hard work had gone into that building, so much prayer. It had been our home in the mountains for years, a lighthouse from which radiated the rays of divine truth, the birthplace of precious souls. Now the light was extinguished, the whole place was in ruins. I thought of the words of Paul, 'We may be knocked down, but we are never knocked out. We are always facing death, but this means that you know more and more of life.' Paul got up and fought on, and so must we.

Chapter Eleven

Translation of the Living Word

The door to Kabylia was closed. God had permitted that part of his work to be brought to a standstill. The Bible Society knew that I had translated the four gospels into the Berber dialect used in Lesser Kabylia, and that this translation had been very well received. The local representative of the Bible Society had asked me, just before hostilities started, to be responsible for the revision of the Kabyle New Testament. There were many unfortunate mistakes in the first translation, and these had to be corrected with the help of the nationals. God set me free from my very busy life as an evangelist in order that I might devote my time to the even more important work of translation for which he had been equipping me during the past thirty years. How often had I sat in a coffee house and noted the expressions used by the men, or hidden behind a bush and listened to successive groups of men returning from the market. Their voices came over so clearly in the still atmosphere of the mountain.

A committee was formed of national believers and missionaries from a wide area. The only snag was that committee meetings meant travelling over roads made dangerous by the opposing sides in the civil war. Once more I was utterly cast upon God for protection. Many of God's servants deemed it foolhardy to travel at such a time, but for me there was no choice. If the consultants over a large area were to be contacted, and they were unable or unwilling to travel, then I must go to them. But how? Should a servant of God travel under the protection of a military escort? Or should I continue to take those long perilous journeys trusting in a living God to protect me? Surely the attitude of Ezra should be mine! 'I was ashamed to ask the king for soldiers and horsemen to protect us from enemies on the road, because we had told the king; "The good hand of our God is on everyone who looks to him."' The Kabyles were all fully aware of my attitude and accepted it as logical. Down through the years a Muslim who became a Christian had always to face the possibility of death. As a Christian missionary I was never an apostate, and was therefore immune to threats to my life on this level. Now the glorious opportunity had come to adopt an attitude of strict neutrality, of absolute dependance on God, and to give practical truth that the God who I served was able to deliver.—'He will deliver'—but if not? The possibility had to be faced. If God did not deliver from death, I knew that I should go to be with my Lord.

The journey to Les Ouadhias necessitated a special pass. Two roads leading to the area were so dangerous that they were forbidden to all but military vehicles. One road remained open. The evidences of war were on every hand. There were block houses in every village from which guns peered through, look-out towers, military patrols, the rattle of machine guns, in the distance the boom of heavy artillery, the roar of low-flying aircraft and helicopters. After six hour's travelling over those dangerous roads, I reached the mission station in the heart of Kabylia where two single missionary sisters were bravely carrying on. The house was situated outside the protected area of the village. Every window and door was sandbagged to give protection from flying bullets. A new house was under construction, and it was there that I was to spend the night.

There were no locks to the doors, and in this house I was to sleep and work during the day.

'You cannot lock yourself in at night,' said Soeur Hélène as she showed me my room. 'The Kabyle men who are decorating the house will be sleeping below in another room. Fighting goes on all round—right through the night.'

'What are those small holes in that wall?' I enquired.

'Oh, those are just bullet holes. Last night one came in here and went out there, and the other one lodged in that pillar.'

Soeur Hélène left, and I bent down to line up the two holes where the bullet had come in and gone out. It would have passed about two inches over my head. I turned the bed round the other way!

It was ten o'clock. The boom of artillery shelling a distant village, the rattle of machine guns close at hand, and the plop plop of shotguns from the Nationalists, made sleep almost impossible. Quite suddenly a pack of jackals started to yelp and howl. Jackals? So many and so near? I got out of bed and crept across to the shutters, and peered out into the darkness. I could just discern in the pale moonlight the dusky forms of the men preparing to attack the military post. So these were the jackals! The long night passed and the morning came.

During the daylight hours the work of revision went on. 'The Son of Man came'—shall we change that word for man? Is Jesus the son of a man? Should it not rather be, '*Emmis m bounadem,*' linking him thus with the human race?

'Of course that is much the better word,' said my blind consultant.

'Then why did you Kabyles not point out some of these wrong words before?'

'We always thought that the missionary knew better than we did.'

I worked on with Jules from early morning until

sunset, almost without a break, and as we worked the battle raged. The last committee meeting for the Kabyle New Testament was held at Azazga, right in the midst of the war zone. No missionary or consultant would leave his home to travel by public or private transport. It was far too risky. Buses were burned out, trains derailed every day. Nevertheless the meeting had to be held, before I could complete the final manuscript and send it off to headquarters. Blind Jules said that he would only attend the conference if I went with the car and fetched him. I shall never forget that long journey of fifty kilometers on a Sunday afternoon. Not a soul was to be seen. Even military patrols were absent, and the bridges apparently unguarded; yet the sense of danger, of evil, lurked everywhere. Then on to Azazga with another Kabyle consultant, up to a Kabyle village to collect another. Final decisions were taken, the manuscript adapted and despatched, and the proofs awaited. One question was uppermost in our minds. 'Would the revised Kabyle New Testament ever be used?' Was the Bible Society justified in spending the money? It was finally printed in 1959, but for several years the edition did not sell. The future was so uncertain. Then suddenly, just ten years after independence was declared, the whole edition sold out in three months. Our work was not in vain.

A short furlough followed. Oh! the relief to be right away from the tensions of war, away from the searchlights that swept the whole village throughout the night, the hideous howl of the wounded dog, the yapping of the jackals, the lone call of the owl; every sound having its signification for the rebels and the population. Away, from the rattle of a machine gun as someone broke the curfew and paid the price; away, from the bursting bombs, the cries of tortured prisoners . . . The furlough passed quickly and Africa called. Should we go back? Surely our growing children needed us?

If you had been to Muslim lands,
Where suffering men stretched out their hands
To plead, yet no one understands;
Would you go back, would you?

If you had trod through Afric's sand
Your hand within the Saviour's hand,
And knew he'd called you to that land;
Would you go back, would you?

If you had seen the women bear
Their heavy loads with none to share,
Had heard them weep with none to care;
Would you go back, would you?

If you had seen the Christian die,
And stand for Christ when none was nigh,
Had seen him smile and say 'Goodbye'—
Would you go back, would you?

Yet still they wait, a listless throng,
Longing for one to right their wrong,
When shall despair be turned to song?
We're going back. Would you?[1]

So back we went, and what a welcome we received! On the night of our arrival at Lafayette there was a terrible storm and a cloudburst. The small stream which flowed through the Hammam became a raging torrent. It rose twenty feet high, sweeping over the bridge in the center of the village. The bridge collapsed and was swept away, one whole section of the village was engulfed and some people lost their lives. I went down to see what was happening and arrived just in time to see the last wall of our small Hall collapse and slide into the river. Everything disappeared in the raging torrent.

God had allowed his work to continue until this fourth

[1] Adapted; author unknown

year of the fight for independence. For two and a half
years it had been situated in 'no man's land' between
the areas occupied by the opposing forces. To visit it
I had to obtain a special pass and travel beyond the last
French outpost. The Hammam itself was visited by
the rebels every night. Numbers attending the clinics
had been slightly less than in normal years, but the
Word of God had been a comfort to so many. Now the
Hall, where for nearly thirty four years the gospel had
been preached, was destroyed; carried away by the
hand of God. It seemed another knock-out blow. There
was no possibility of recommencing work either at
Hammam or at Beni Ourtilane. The army authorities
refused us permission to rebuild, or even to erect a
temporary structure. Within a few days of the flood,
fighting broke out in Hammam, all the men were im-
prisoned, and it would have been impossible to continue the work.

Until this time my life had been remarkably full.
Each week as many as twenty or twenty-five groups of
people had come under my ministry. Now I was free to
give most of time to the work for which God had been
preparing me for years. He makes no mistakes. His
timing is perfect. Again, at the request of the British
and Foreign Bible Society, I undertook to supervise a
committee for the adaptation of the Moroccan Bible for
use throughout North Africa. This adaptation again
entailed long journeys by road, with an even closer
sense of the Lord's presence and keeping power.
During my long absences from home Pearl bravely
carried on the work at Lafayette. What stories she had
to tell!

On one occasion one thousand men were suddenly
billeted in our village. The officer insisted that some
must live in our home, or in the Gospel Hall. Pearl was
alone and I was in Algiers. Twenty rough soldiers were
duly installed in the Hall. Throughout the night the
sentry tramped up and down the yard. In the Hall the

men slept, ate and smoked. How could Pearl continue classes and meetings in such an atmosphere and under such conditions? Each week two hundred Muslim children were coming to learn God's Word. The boys insisted that they were men, and should not be turned out of their *jamâ* (mosque). They assured Pearl that they were not going to be intimidated by French soldiers, so, with men of the French army in one part of the Hall, they sang all the French hymns that they knew. Pearl gave the talk in the same language, and some hearts at least were touched. She went outside and found one of the men listening with tears in his eyes.

A few days later the whole of the Muslim male population of Lafayette was behind barbed-wire entanglements, surrounded by soldiers with fierce dogs and tommy guns. They were kept there for more than a week with no shelter; hungry, dirty, chilled to the bone, cowed and embittered. They thought of their unprotected homes, of the uncouth soldiers going from house to house, sometimes emptying all the food on the floor; wheat, barley, figs and oil, then pouring paraffin on the heap of food and setting fire to it. A tragedy indeed for poor hungry people. They were accused, rightly or wrongly, of feeding the rebels during the night. These men thought of their women, who were now at the mercy of the military with no one to protect them. Suddenly they stared. Along the street came a band of soldiers, herding before them a mass of frightened women, who were clutching at their veils and flimsy dresses in a vain attempt to cover themselves and shield their babies. They were accustomed to the absolute privacy of their homes, and now . . . Squads of men went from quarter to quarter of the village driving out the women, who were so reluctant to leave.

A little girl came flying in to Pearl, panting for breath, terrified at all that was happening. 'They are taking all the women, and leaving us girls behind alone.

What can we do? Where can we go? Pray, pray, pray
for us. We know Jesus will save us. He will protect us.
Just pray, pray for us.' Then she dashed off like an
arrow to help her younger sister. To whom could they
turn in their hour of distress but to one who could pray,
to Lalla Jouhra who so often had prayed for them and
with them in their homes?

God's protective care of his servants impressed many
Muslims at this time. They were thinking deeply, but
fear, fear of reprisals, fear of the unknown future,
fear of breaking with Islam, kept them back from full
surrender to the claims of the Lord. The situation
worsened and the whole place was surrounded by
barbed-wire entanglements to keep out the enemy at
night. The rebels cut through the barbed wire and
entered our neighbour's house. The occupant had been
warned and escaped with his life. Everything that he
possessed was piled in a heap in the middle of the floor
and then fired. Then they attacked the French forces,
firing across our back garden. Under such conditions
the work still continued. Every week fifty or more
veiled Muslim women came to the clinic, and listened
to a message from the Bible. They were the mothers of
the children who attended the classes. Boys and girls
came to the classes, even when bombs were falling
half a mile away. Past the sentries they came, their
happy singing in strange contrast to the din of the
helicopters that roared overhead.

The most terrifying experience for Pearl was when
she was alone in the house for a week while I was in
Algiers. Just over fifty yards away was an isolated
military post, manned by a French NCO and a dozen
Arabs. The men were not allowed to retain their arms
at night in case they should rebel. 'Sergeant, come and
look. Listen! The enemy is approaching. Give us our
rifles.' The sergeant left the shelter of his room, was
attacked from behind and hacked to pieces with an axe.
His shrieks and cries pierced the night. The Arab men

defected to the rebel army, taking their arms with them. No one came to the help of the dying man, even though the Gendarmerie was only fifty yards away. How terrifying for Pearl, alone in our home. Yet she was not alone, for he himself has said, 'Never will I leave you; never will I forsake you.' So that she could boldly say, even at such a time, 'I will not be afraid. What can man do to me?' Here was true fellowship in the gospel; Pearl willingly accepting the responsibility for the home and the Lord's work; to enable me to travel on the dangerous roads to complete the translations.

Once again I was asked to head up the committee for the completion of the New Testament in Algerian Arabic. The situation changed overnight. The European settlers themselves now revolted against the French army. In the centre of Algiers they had thrown up barricades, had occupied the whole block of University buildings, and Frenchmen armed with modern weapons faced Frenchmen. Every available soldier of the army was sent to Algiers. The radio proclaimed a state of public emergency. This all happened on the day which we had fixed for the last series of committee meetings! Again I was in a quandary. Dare I make that long journey? It was yet another challenge to faith. Would these translations ever be used? The doors for Christian work were fast closing. '*Madame, votre mari est fou* (Madame, your husband is mad),' said the French people when they heard that I had ventured on the roads. Folly in the eyes of the world, but when God commissions, and calls, then he gives all needed protection and there is really no danger.

Every road junction was closely guarded. Tanks lined the roads overlooking the railway. Troops were everywhere. Convoys cluttered up the roads. 'Halt! Get out of your car. Hands up! Well over your head,' the sentry ordered. A thorough search of the car followed.

'Where are you going?'

'To Algiers.'

'But Algiers is surrounded by troops. You will never be allowed to enter the city. No one is allowed in.'

'I can but try.'

'Well, if you are fool enough to try, you can carry on. Bon voyage! But you will not reach Algiers today.'

I committed the situation to my never-failing Lord. 'Lord, you must get me through. You have never, no never, let me down. Lord, it is your work, not mine. Please just get me there.' I was held up twenty times on that journey, the car was searched, I was searched. Then came the crucial test—Menerville. I passed through the town and then saw the successive control posts, army . . . gendarmes . . . army. There was no doubt about it. Here they really meant business. I slowed down as I reached the first control post, taking my wallet, identity card and travelling permit from my pocket. I could hardly believe my eyes. The sentry waved me on. I was two hundred miles from home. No one knew me. Surely the civilian police would stop me. Incredible though it may seem, they too waved me on. At the third post the sharp harrows which would puncture the tires were all ready to be pulled across the road, but again I was motioned to proceed. I was through the crucial spot, and had not even been asked to show my papers. Just outside Algiers I was directed to stop and a very thorough inspection took place. They suspected my typewriter, but they found no weapons, no grenades, no bombs! I was through. Praise the Lord for that!

Algiers was like a dead city. Glass littered the streets. No one dared to leave the shelter of a building. Many buildings were in ruins, shattered by plastic bombs.

The committee meeting started only half-an-hour behind scheduled time.

We worked on steadily for a week while every day men were murdered on the road outside. One day the gutters on both sides ran with human blood. Fifteen schools went up in flames in a single night. Every hour beautiful villas were blasted. Algiers was a city of death—of dying, despairing men and women. Yet the servants of God worked at the translation of the Living Word, the Word which was to bring cheer and comfort, life and salvation to a liberated Algeria.

A week later, on my way back home, I arrived at Bordj bou Arreridj.

'Where have you been all this week?' my fellow missionaries asked me.

'I have been in Algiers working on the New Testament.'

'That is virtually impossible, for no one has been allowed to travel to Algiers during the whole week. No one got through the day that you travelled.'

'Where were they turned back?'

'At Menerville.'

It was the very place, the only place, where my papers had not been examined, the place where the authorities had waved me on. Can anyone doubt the power, wisdom and love of our God, the supreme Authority?

Conditions at Lafayette became ever more severe. There were increasing restrictions on the work. Men were afraid to visit us. The translations were complete. Then came an invitation to visit the Chad Republic, with the aim of forwarding the evangelisation of Muslims in that land. To pack our belongings and leave the home where our children had been born and reared meant a real sacrifice. Yet it was plain that the door for any effective service in Algeria was temporarily closed. In the Lord's mercy it could be reopened, but the time of waiting could be profitably used for God's glory in the Chad. So to the Chad we went.

The story of those years is told in *Streams in the Sahara*. Having spent two years there, Pearl returned alone to an independent Algeria to explore the possibilities of resuming work there. We had left a man and his family to occupy our home and act as caretaker. Harzi, an officer of the Algerian Army of Liberation had obtained the keys of our hall and our home by threatening the lady missionary with whom we left them. He took over the house, threatening to kill the caretaker. To save his life he fled, leaving Harzi in complete control. He lived in our home and let out the hall to others. Many things had been stolen, and everywhere was filthy. He had refused to pay the rates or to pay for the electricity that he had used. We informed the Sub-Prefect of our desire to return to our home, and recommence the Lord's work. Harzi informed us that if anyone dared to set foot on the property or to come to see us, he would not hesitate to take his gun and use it. There were guns in our bedroom and in my study. He had himself been responsible for the death of scores of innocent people in the area; and there is no doubt at all, that had we returned, he would have carried out his threat. This time it was the lives of others which were endangered, and not our own. The Sub-Prefect asked us not to spend a single night in our home, as he could not answer for the consequences if we did.

In order to show this cruel godless man that I did not fear him, I returned to the house on a later occasion and spent two nights with him there alone. I was not afraid of him, but I would not endanger the lives of others. Finally Harzi purchased the property for a nominal sum; reselling it within a few months and making a tremendous profit. The Lord later dealt with him, as he does with all who oppose his work. Harzi had a tragic accident and for years was an object of pity and scorn. 'There goes the man who attempted to stop God's work,' they said; as the poor wreck of a man passed by. The official who collaborated with him to turn us out died suddenly in the very chair in which he was seated when he stated, 'God almighty has gone to France.'

For the time being at least, our work in Algeria was

finished. The blow was severe. It hurt us to leave, and Pearl suffered acutely, for it was the land of her birth, and we both loved the Kabyle people. God had closed the door in Algeria, and we left for Central Africa to translate yet another New Testament, and to supply precision tools such as the French-Arabic dictionary for evangelists, tracts, a hymn book and an approach course for African evangelists who desired to reach the Muslims.[1]

[1] This course has now been adapted and is published by Moody Press under the title *Share your faith with a Muslim.*

Chapter Twelve

Dawning—A New Era?

In 1962, amid scenes of wild rejoicing, the long seven-year war came to an end, and Algeria was granted Independence. To save their lives, over a million Européans left the country, most of them abandoning their homes, furniture, property and all that they possessed. Many people were convinced that, when Independence came, all Christian work would automatically cease; but for a very short time, the Algerian authorities granted religious liberty to the very small Christian minority, and God's work continued. Alas, this impartial attitude was only maintained for a few years, but all can rejoice that during that period there was an evident working of the Holy Spirit in the lives of many young people.

For ten years after independence our daughter bravely continued the Lord's work at Tazmalt in the interior of the country. She had continued to visit the sick during the rebellion and over one hundred had been shot dead in the village itself. If she was visiting a sick person and shooting started, a nearby door would open, and she would shelter till the immediate danger had past. She is a qualified nurse and was overwhelmed by the crowds of women who attended the clinic. The classes that she held for children increased tremendously in numbers and she was literally exhausted by the amount of work. The people themselves were hardened to the gospel, and while they appreciated the social services and were most friendly, any attempt on the part of a young person to break from Islam was persistently opposed. Indeed many of the elderly Kabyles insisted that they did believe in the Lord Jesus, but followed the religion of Islam!

When our work of translation in the Chad was complete, Pearl and I spent six months in a Kabyle village, and we found that there was a persistent refusal on the part of professing Christians to go all the way with the Lord Jesus. In striking contrast a more liberal spirit prevailed in the towns. Friday prayers in the mosques were well attended by the older generation, but Islam was losing its grip on the young. The Koran was being taught increasingly, and in many schools all the lessons were in Arabic, but there was a certain liberty.

I faced the biggest challenge of my life when I was asked by the Baptists to be padre in their camps for children and young people for a period of three years.

The camps were authorised by the Muslim Government and were open to inspection at any time, but we had liberty to teach and study the Bible. Let me describe a typical camp of teenage boys and girls. Every one of the group of sixty was from a Muslim home. I looked into the faces of these keen young people as they gathered under the pine trees close to the Mediterranean sea. Fifty yards away was a holiday camp run by Algerians. They were singing worldly Muslim songs, and their voices came across on the night air. Many of the strapping young men in our group were taller than myself, some of them convinced Muslims, others out for fun and a good time. Light flippant girls mingled with their more serious sisters. I was to be responsible for passing on more than forty messages during the next three weeks; and I was answerable to God for the future of these young lives. I faced an impossible task, humanly speaking. Prayer was the only answer.

'Will any keen Algerian Christians who would like

to join me in prayer, please come to my small hut this evening?' I expected, I hoped, that two, or perhaps three, would come. Thirty-two turned up! They sat on my bed, on the table, on a form and stood two deep round the walls. 'If you ask—I will do,' was the promise. They did ask, and God worked. That year in that one camp twenty-one Muslims trusted the Saviour. How wonderful in *any* land, but in independent Algeria . . . !

Khalidja was a timid girl of fourteen. She had two friends who were radiant Christians, and they were trying to win her for Christ. To them she confided that she really did want to believe; but she was so afraid of her father. 'He will whip me and beat me, if ever I become a Christian.' The day came when she could hold out no longer. Just after dinner she came to my hut with her two friends and very simply, yet very sincerely, committed her life to him who is able to save. Then she went off to siesta during the heat of the day. At three o'clock she was back at my hut. She said, 'Uncle, I went right off to sleep and I had a vivid dream. A horrid man came to me, a man with diabolical looks. He said to me, "Khalidja, what have you done? You have left your religion to follow Jesus Christ. I will never, never leave you until I kill you, or until you come back to Islam, and if you don't I shall do this and that to you—you will suffer unspeakably. You will be starved and beaten." He described all that is done to an apostate girl. Who was he, Uncle?' she asked. 'What does it mean?' She was terrified. I could only tell her that the devil himself was trying to turn her back from allegiance to Christ.

Later in the afternoon her two girl friends came along, and with tears in their eyes, said, 'Khalidja has denied the Lord.' She told the other girls that she really did not mean it. She was just pretending.' There was only one resort, prayer. The two girls remained after the prayer meeting that evening to pray for

Khalidja. Each of them prayed, and then I committed her to the Lord. I thought that they would immediately want to join the others at games; but they each prayed again, and yet again. One seldom hears such prayers, and when they come from hearts that only a year before were in bondage to Islam they are full of the music of heaven. 'Lord, show yourself to Khalidja, in all your magnificence, in all your power and glory, in all your beauty and strength. Lord, Satan has shown his hand. If she only sees you, Lord Jesus, she will never go back.' Or again, 'Lord, you have said, "No-one can snatch them out of my hand." Hold her fast, Lord.' Thus these two radiant Christian girls pleaded for their friend. Three days later she again committed her life to the Lord Jesus. She knew full well that her father would give her a beating when he heard that she was a Christian; but with tremendous courage she went to face it.

Every morning the whole group gathered to study the book of Exodus, and the story of redemption. Then we went to the beach for bathing and games. In the evening a simple gospel message was given in Arabic or French. Then there was a brief time of quiet, when each one was invited to consider the claims of the Redeemer. During the following day those who had trusted the Lord Jesus, or who desired spiritual help, came along for a quiet talk.

It was Sunday evening. In a clearing of the forest the camp fire burned brightly. A young fellow of seventeen gave his testimony. 'God greatly blessed me when I came to camp last year and I trusted the Saviour. Then I went back home and met with terrible opposition; they tore my Bible to pieces, they hit me and cursed me. I went down to the depths of despair. Everything was black. My faith went. But God in his grace has spoken to me again this year. I have been greatly helped and blessed. I am going back home to follow my Lord all the way. It may well mean that they will turn me out of home. I know that I shall meet with violent opposition. Perhaps they may try and poison me. Pray for me that I may stand and that God will keep me true.' God graciously helped him and the following year he returned as a camp monitor. By his steadfast loyalty, his self discipline, his solid spirituality during a period of six weeks of intensive effort, he proved himself a stalwart servant of God. (That happened nine years ago. He has since qualified as a teacher and is serving the Lord and living a consistent Christian life.)

Wherever there is a work of God it will be challenged. As the confidence of the young people was won, they felt able to express their doubts and their difficulties. The lad who opposed most was the son of an ardent Nationalist who had been killed in the war. This boy later wrote to me, 'I went away from that camp feeling physically ill. I could not forget the messages from God's Word, the daily Bible studies. I remembered the faithful way in which we were told of sins that we did not even know were wrong; the warm earnestness with which our salvation from hell was sought, and above all, the prayers of Algerian Christians. God worked in my heart, and *now I am saved* and I want everyone to know it.' What a triumph of grace in the heart of this Saul of Tarsus, that, four months after leaving the camp he was saved!

The opposition was even more pronounced the following year in the camp for adolescents. Once again over sixty teenagers gathered, mostly those of the fifteen to sixteen year age group. This time the leaders and co-leaders of each group were Christians from Muslim homes. They themselves were only a year or two older than the young people for whom they were responsible. It was wonderful to find young Algerian Christians willing to spend their holidays in winning others for the Lord Jesus.

The pattern was very similar to that of the previous year. Studies in Genesis every morning, group studies on various subjects in the afternoon, and each evening a clear gospel message. Some of these talks were given by the young Algerians. They also conducted the revision of the previous day's lesson. They led family prayers each morning, and during the camp each of these young workers was asked to give his, or her, testimony to the saving grace of God.

'To whom might the Lord have referred when he said, "Beware of false prophets?"' This rather provocative question was put to the groups for individual and collective study. The leader of each study group was then asked to give the findings of the group. The girls' groups started. 'Seventh Day Adventists,' said one group. 'Jehovah's Witnesses,' said the second. 'Mohammed,' said the third. I hastened on to the answers from the boys' groups; deliberately turning a deaf ear to the murmurs of disapproval coming from some people. Then the voice of a keen Algerian boy was heard, 'Uncle, did you not notice the reaction to one reply? It is obvious that there are some here who do not agree that Mohammed was a false prophet. I should like to prove from the Scriptures that he was, because he denied the deity of Christ.' He proceeded to do so.

Immediately there was a sharp division in the camp. It was now evident to all that no one can profess to believe in the Lord Jesus and maintain a secret allegiance to Mohammed. The girl who had read out the answer of her group was told that she ought to be ashamed, and that she would be killed when they returned to Oran. Another boy started to sing a parody of a chorus 'I am so glad that Mohammed saved me.' He knew that it was a deliberate lie, for the poor lad was fully aware that Mohammed had not, and could not save him, but he felt that in loyalty to Mohammed he must express his feelings. Then a message was found written across the dining room table, 'You are all hide-bound, and do not know what you are talking about. You do not believe either in Jesus or in Mohammed.' It was obvious that a crisis had been reached. It could be met only by prayer. That evening my bedroom was packed to capacity. Elsewhere the leaders gathered to pray.

Two days later, when all signs of the rebellious spirit had passed, I had a quiet talk with each of the ringleaders, and especially with the lad who had written the insulting message. It was not easy to continue the gospel messages in such an atmosphere, but the impact was even more direct. The question box was in continual use. From an Algerian Christian girl came the challenge, 'Will any Muslim come forward and in five minutes tell us of any one thing that Mohammed has done for him, that Jesus Christ has not done for us.' No one offered to do so. From Muslims came, 'Why does the Koran speak of Jesus Christ, and the Bible does not mention Mohammed?' and 'How can we be quite sure that the Bible is true?'

In several families three persons trusted the Saviour. It was evident that God was answering their prayers for Christian families. Day after day young people came through, until sixteen had professed conversion in that one camp, ten girls and six fellows. By the second week it was obvious that there were more Christians than Muslims, so the messages of the last four days were on discipleship, the Lordship of Christ and practical Christian living.

The last evening came, and we were all seated round the camp fire for the final message. One after another of the Algerians told of a new-found life in Christ. By the light of the fire I stood to give the final message, the last gospel message that I was to give on Algerian soil. 'All day long I have held out my hands to a disobedient and obstinate people.' No appeal was made, but we were all fully aware that this was the last opportunity for some. All of us were to rise at four-thirty the next morning for the long journey home. I closed in prayer, and as I turned from the circle, a tall figure approached. He was the ringleader of the Muslims, the fellow who had written the insulting message. He had come to say 'Goodbye'. As he kissed me, first on one cheek, and then the other, I said to him, 'So you are leaving, having made no decision?' 'I have made my decision,' was the quiet reply. 'I have come to Christ.' We read the Scriptures together and then knelt in prayer. Once more that little hut was the scene of deep repentance, as the erstwhile fanatical Muslim told Jesus Christ that he surrendered unconditionally to him, and accepted him as Lord and Saviour.

What happens when a young convert returns home? Let us follow one: 'Dad, did you know that in Nuwara's group at camp, someone said that Mohammed is a false prophet?'

Nuwara was sitting at table with her brother and sister, her mother and father. When he heard this, her father was almost beside himself. In fury he turned to his seventeen year old daughter and said, 'I hope that you had nothing to do with that answer?' Calmly she replied, 'Father, I was the only one to make the statement.' His fury knew no bounds. He took Nuwara into the next room, and thrashed her for at least ten minutes. The next day he told her, 'You had better go to your Grandmother's house to live. I don't ever want to see you again. All my love for you has gone. Go!' How easy it would have been for Nuwara to have remained silent, to hide her light, to deny the words in order to escape that cruel beating, the shame and the suffering. She later wrote to me:

Dear Uncle, forgive this delay in writing. I chose not to write before, for I wanted to be quite sure just what was going to happen. I told my father that I was a Christian, but he did not take me seriously. He laughed it off. Then my brother told what I had said about Mohammed. You can imagine how unhappy I was after my father had beaten me, and had said those cruel words. I was on the point of turning back, and giving up. Then I remembered that you told me that with my strong character, God wanted me for a leader. I pray daily for the Christians of Algeria. Dear Uncle, you know that I am deeply grieved to see people all round me dying without forgiveness, and unprepared for death. I long to see the Church of Jesus Christ established here in Algeria. Then all Algerians could perhaps hear the gospel, and find the way of salvation. That is my daily prayer. I always carry the New Testament with me in my satchel, and I have been able to lead two other girls in my class to the Saviour. Their names are—— and ——. They will soon be writing to tell you.

A further letter stated:

Dear Uncle, I am so glad to tell you that my parents are no longer persecuting me as they did. I believe that this is a miracle brought about by the Lord. Latterly I have read my Bible a lot, and I am dazzled and fascinated by the power and the richness of the promises. Every morning I feel that I simply must thank the Great Giver of all good whom I adore. The more I read the Bible, the more I discover that Christ is too good for us; for we do not deserve all this. He suffered for us. Did Mohammed do this? No. That's what I tell all my friends, who think that I am ridiculous. I want to tell you something which may make you laugh. I should so much like to die for Christ, in order to say, 'Thank you' to him. Of course, it is hard to think this, but when I reflect on all that he has done for me . . . !

A few weeks later I received another letter from her of which extracts only can be given:

Dear Uncle, I have tremendous news for you which will certainly give you much pleasure. Part of my prayers have been answered. I knew that a miracle was about to happen . . . Every Thursday afternoon we come together for a meeting. We pray together, read and sing. I do my best to explain a passage of the Bible. We are only seven in number, but it is just wonderful. Now I am coming to the surprise. One day my mother came up and she heard us singing. She came in, took a spare chair, and listened to the end. Then I switched over and explained the passage in Arabic. She was really touched, and since then she has never missed one of these meetings. I am sure that Christ is working in her heart to the full. She has told me that the promises given to Christians are so wonderful and beautiful that she wants to hook on to them. So I have understood many things . . . ever since, I do not cease to thank the Lord for his help, for I feel that he is with me. I want you to give me some advice, and some ideas so that I know what to say during these little meetings. I find that it is really quite hard.

Thus in widely separated towns, God has his witnesses who, in the face of opposition are winning others to a living faith in Christ. The choice for them is clear. To hide their light, and remain secret disciples; or to be brave enough to confess their Lord, to stand firm and suffer, and to win others for the Saviour.

Chapter Thirteen

The Camp for Algerian Christians

In addition to the camps for children and teenagers that were held during that three year period, a camp was planned for adolescents who had professed conversion. I was confronted with a challenge as soon as I arrived. The fifty young Algerians were of both sexes, and their ages ranged from fourteen to twnty three. For the next fortnight they were to mix freely, in a land where girls and women have always been segregated. On arrival I had been asked to give this mixed company a straight talk on morality and sex ethics. But to speak of sex in a public meeting in Algeria is absolutely taboo. To mention the word 'adultery' in a village meeting in Kabylia is to lose the entire audience of men. I was very much cast on the Lord for that opening message. Yet it paved the way for what followed. In this time of transition, of breaking with past traditions, both girls and fellows were faced with many problems. In an amazing way these young people confided to me their problems and quite openly asked:

'Is it wrong for a girl to think of marriage?'

'What sort of a girl should a fellow choose in a country where the girl is usually chosen for him?'

'Should a Christian girl marry a Muslim?'

'What if she is compelled to do so?'

'Should a Christian girl attend a Muslim wedding and put on the henna dye?'

Fatima is a Kabyle missionary and has three children. She confided, 'It is wonderful to see the way you have so quickly won the confidence of the young people. They talk to you as if you were their father; more than that, for they would not dare to speak of some of these subjects with their own parents. How do you do it?'

I had found the answer to that question in Paul's plea to the Galatian Christians, 'Become like me, for I became like you.' I assured my fellow workers that if we wanted these young people to become like us in Christian faith and doctrine, we must first become like them by putting ourselves in their place and attempting to understand them. We must share their problems, suffering with them, giving them the benefit of our knowledge of the Scriptures and our experience of God's faithfulness. Such work is costly, and my pillow was often wet with tears as during the night I battled with the problems confronting these dear young Christians, who are faced with continual ostracism and opposition in their homes. I had stood up to stones, danger and opposition for Christ's sake; and through the years God had delivered me, but I had always been able to return to the love and sympathy of my helpmeet and the shelter of my home. But for these young people there could be no withdrawal. The opposition was sustained and continual. I did not hesitate to give them the teaching of Scripture. There must be no divided loyalties, Christ must be Lord of all. The cost of discipleship was high, the world must be renounced, and self crucified. The teaching of Paul in Galatians left no room for choice. A visitor to the camp from France was overheard to say, 'Never before have we heard the truths of discipleship, of Christian discipline and of fidelity to Christ, at whatever cost, so plainly taught. Yet they take it, for all he says is with such love that they listen, count the cost, accept, and are prepared to follow their Lord—all the way.

For an hour and a half each morning we studied the epistle to the Galatians, and found that the teaching exactly fitted their spiritual needs. Later in the day we separated into six groups for a closer study of the passage. Each student had to write down the answer to five questions based on the chapter that we had studied, then the answers were summarised by the group leader, and finally shared with the whole camp. Their deep exercise of heart was evident from their questions:

'Is it really a sin for a Christian to observe the Fast of Ramadhan?'

'If our parents compel us to fast what should we do? obey our parents and go against God's Word and against our conscience or . . . ?'

'Should we eat the meat of the sacrifice offered at the Feast of Sheep?'

'What must one do when he has sinned inadvertently, through ignorance?'

The crowning moment of the day for most of us was the prayer meeting. 'Lord, there are some people who say that it is impossible for a Muslim to be converted and to become a Christian. That never again will there be Christian churches in this Muslim land. But, Lord, you can see that all of us here this evening are from Muslim homes. We love you, we believe in you. We are the tangible evidence that you can save Muslims. You have saved us. We are here as members of your Church, the first of many who will believe in you in this land. We are the pioneers of the new churches in Algeria. Lord, we are the proof that the devil lies. Lord, go on to do a deep work in us and through us everywhere in this land.'

There were fervent 'Amens' as this young Christian closed his prayer. Forty five young Algerians bowed in prayer beneath the pine trees. Fellows and girls sat on the carpet of pine needles in a large circle as the darkness fell, and one after another they poured out their hearts to God in the above strain, sharing in fervent, earnest prayer. Their evening meal over, they were at liberty to amuse themselves, but instead they chose each evening to gather for prayer. The prayers continued:

'Lord, save our parents. We know that you want to save whole families. Lord, we are the first in our families to believe. Lord, how wonderful it would be to have a Christian home! A home where we could sit and quietly read your Word every day without having it snatched from our hands and pages torn out. A home where we could quietly pray without interference; where we could openly sing these lovely hymns and choruses whenever we wanted to, instead of being cursed and shouted at and hit. A home where we could find sympathy and love, and not opposition and blows. Lord, please save our families and give us Christian homes.

There were no long prayers. Nearly everyone present prayed, and the burden of each was that, when they returned to their homes, God would keep them faithful in the face of the continual and severe opposition. They prayed that he would strengthen the girls who had just gone home from a previous camp, and who had been beaten when they informed their parents that they were Christians.

'Lord, make me to desire joyfully thy will and give me the strength to do it.'

I bowed my head in humble worship and adoration as I listened to these fervent prayers. Here, indeed, was concrete evidence that nothing is too hard for God. This is what I prayed for, the aim of our labours for so many years. A band of over fifty Christian young people in an independent Muslim land. How great is our God!

Sadik had come to the Lord the previous year. Then a lad of seventeen, he had matured considerably and was often seen with his open Bible talking to one or more Muslim men outside the camp, seeking ardently to win them for his Lord.

Fereeda was in revolt against God. She had asked God time and again to incline her parents to consent to her becoming a Christian, but they had adamantly refused. She had prayed so hard, so intently, but there seemed to be no answer. She had done her best to become a Christian, but it was useless to try to live for God in her home. Her deep resentment and deep-seated rebellion were evident on her face. It was useless to try and talk with her. But the Lord triumphed in her life. She surrendered to the Lord, and a few days after returning home she wrote to her friend, 'I wanted to tell mother and on July 30th God gave me the courage to do so. I told her how the Lord Jesus had saved me. She reproached me bitterly. She shouts at me whenever she sees me reading my Bible. When I spoke to her about the Lord Jesus she grew mad with anger, and treated me as a *kafra*, a heathen girl. She told me to go, as I must no longer remain with her in the same house. She said, "I don't want to stay in the same house with you when you have changed your religion." I told her that the Lord Jesus is the only way to God, and that he alone gave himself for our sins. She hit me again and again. She invited me to repent and to return to Islam. I told her that every Muslim is under law, and therefore condemned. If he does not accept Jesus as his personal Saviour he will remain under the condemnation of God. I told mother that I could no longer conscientiously observe the Fast of Ramadhan, as it is part of a religion of works; only if compelled to do so would I fast. But she does not understand. "You were born Muslim and you will remain Muslim," she says. I beg you to pray for me. Pray that my mother will understand, and that I may be able to convince her from the Word of God. Pray that God will strengthen me in spite of all the wrongs done to me.'

She wrote to me a fortnight later saying that she was experiencing God's keeping power. She wrote, 'My mother is unchanged. She now tries to persuade me to be a Christian in secret, without telling anyone of my faith, but that is impossible. She went to the mosque for Friday prayers. The *imam* (religious leader) spoke to them of the Lord Jesus and the miracles that he performed. She told me, 'We do believe in the Lord Jesus, but our religion is purer than yours.' Mother now tries to speak to me kindly, but all I know is that a Christian girl who has pledged herself to follow the Lord Jesus must never, no *never*, turn back. It was very hard to endure all the hardships and difficulties during the first days. I asked the Lord to help me and I can say that until now he has always answered my prayers. Even though the persecution has not stopped, he has given me the courage to bear it.'

It was the closing night of the camp. The camp fire was burning and several Algerian Christians had given striking evidence of the way in which Christ had transformed their lives. Then a young man of eighteen, speaking from a full heart, and with deep emotion as he referred to his parents, tried to prepare his fellow countrymen for the fiery trial that awaited them when they returned to their homes. Unhappily his words lose some of their power by translation.

'God is powerful. I should like to say to those fellows and girls who have accepted Christ, and who are about to return to their homes. I accepted Christ into my heart, but it was a considerable time before I told my parents. I am sure that I did wrong in not telling them before. Really, the people whom we should love and cherish more than anyone else in the world are our parents. If we desire to speak of Christ to our friends, we must speak to our parents first of all. I myself hesitated to do this because I was afraid. Why was I afraid? I was afraid, that's all. But God wanted me to speak to my parents, and it was God who decided that I should do so. I was forced to do it. One day I was faced with the choice. I could not go back. Either I could deny my faith in Christ, or I could confess him. Only these two ways were open to me. I should like to tell you what happened afterwards. I do not want to say this to you to boast in any way, or to say to you, ''Look, this is what I did.'' No, but just to prove to you the power of God in an Algerian Christian. People have a tendency to say—and even Christian leaders say it—that a Muslim can never become a Christian. I say, ''I was a Muslim and now I am a Christian.'' I should like to say what God can do in a Muslim who becomes a Christian. When you confess Christ, of course, your family no longer speaks to you. After that they no longer give you food, or do your washing. That is not enough. The next thing is the mosque, and you will be called before the *imams.* Some of them will ply you with questions with a certain psychology, others will be more brutal. But what is hardest of all to bear is the impression that one has of having betrayed a mother's love, a father's love. Several times I have cried in front of my mother when she has told me all that she had suffered for my sake. That impression one has of having betrayed her love. That is what chokes you. It is terrible in the extreme. Something that you just cannot bear. You feel so small. You feel such a terrible sadness, that you just want to disappear altogether. Then it is that God shows his love. That is when he shows his power. Over and over again I have been tempted to say to my mother, just to please her (yes, I know that this is very superficial), to tell her that I was no longer a Christian. But God was always there. He always arranged everything for the best. He gave me strength to go on with Christ. Several times I have been in the hands of the leaders in the mosque, and there they used the Koran, they tried logic, showing how in Algeria it is much easier to follow what the Koran says, as it is the Word of God. I reached the utmost limit, really it was the limit. I was on the point of doubting what I had seen in the light. But God gave me the answers and delivered me. I want to say this to you, my friends, "You must never doubt in the darkness what you have seen in the light." In this camp you have seen that the Bible is the Word of God. You are going home, and I am sure that in one way or another you will be tempted to your utmost limits to doubt the Word of God. Satan is powerful, he is the prince of this world, but he is not almighty. You know in your hearts that Christ is the Saviour, and you will go back home and by every means in their power they will try and turn you back. But I plead with you, try and come back to all that you have learned in this camp; that Christ is the only Saviour and the Bible is the Word of God. Never doubt in the darkness what you have learned in the light, and Christ will bless you, and he will give you strength. He will make it possible for you to triumph in every trial and temptation. I say this because that is what happened to me, and God has shown his power through me. I would never have thought that I could have stood against the imams, as I did, with all their books, but by the *power of God*—and all glory to him—that is what happened.'

There were many who joined with me in saying, 'Praise the Lord!' as he sat down. Algeria needs men like that, and God is preparing them.

So we said 'Goodbye' to each other, and they went home to face the bitter opposition and continual persecution, while I went back to the love of my dear ones, to Christian fellowship and ease. Independent witness to the changed lives of some of these young people was given later in a letter from a Salvation Army officer to a friend.

'Dahabiya has completely changed. It is a pleasure to see the way in which she is opening up. Rahma must accept marriage to a Muslim or be turned from home. She refuses. "I am a Christian, I will *never* marry a Muslim." Halima has brought me her Bible. Her brother wants to burn it. Truly the devil is mad with rage. A good sign . . . but these poor young people!'

Rahma was told by her school teacher to pray Muslim prayers. She refused and was caned before the whole class.

The Lord took Abd al Kader from the camp to a desert oasis, where he is the only Christian. Converted a year ago, he has made tremendous progress in his spiritual life since the camp.

Yamina trusted the Lord as Saviour, came to the camp and made a full commitment to him. When she returned home she was faced with many problems, even although her parents were not opposed. Should she cut herself off completely from her family and worldly firends? The test came when she was invited to go to the women's baths with a girl friend who was about to be married. She knew it would be a time of merriment, when dancing and some rather lewd practices would be observed. She prayed and felt that the Lord would have her go. Acutely aware of her position as a Christian, she withdrew from her friends who approached her and asked why she would no longer dance with them. Her confession of Christ as Lord involved her in scorn, ridicule and suffering. As she looked on the misconduct of her friends, her own heart was deeply moved in gratitude to the one who had saved her from such things, and the tears quietly flowed down her cheeks. Another friend approached her with a taunt, 'It is obvious that you are unhappy. Come on in.' Yamina replied, 'I am not weeping because I am unhappy. On the contrary I have a deep inner joy of which you know nothing, the joy and peace that only God can give. I am weeping because of the excesses to which you commit yourselves.' The friend left her to continue her merriment with her Muslim sisters; but ten minutes later she beckoned to Yamina. When they were alone, she said, 'I want you to tell me how I can find the peace and joy that you have.' Yamina produced her Bible and directed her to faith in the Lord Jesus. 'Can I borrow this wonderful book?' said her friend. That night she went round to Yamina's house and accepted the Lord Jesus as her Saviour.

How many of these have gone on with the Lord? It is quite impossible to say with any certainty. Most of those that have been mentioned are still living Christian lives, and several are serving him in different countries. It is obvious that a Christian girl who has been forcibly married to a Muslim is under tremendous pressure, she is cut off from all Christian fellowship and finds it impossible to communicate by letter. Small wonder that some go back in the face of the fierce opposition. Merzouga did. She returned from camp to face ostracism and opposition. She had been so keen for the Lord. Her brother beat her day after day and threatened to kill her if she did not renounce her faith in Christ. She went to work in a Muslim hospital, and lost her love for the Lord. She even turned against other Christians and denounced them. Fervent prayer was made on her behalf in Algeria and England. She came back to Christ. I was able to spend an hour with her in Algeria after she had returned to the Lord. She prayed, 'Lord give me back that ardour, that audacity to speak to others about you, even in the face of opposition. I once had it and I've lost it.' That simple prayer hit me hard. How much do I know of that keen ardour to witness for my Lord in the face of opposition?

Communications with suffering Christians in other lands may cease as letters are intercepted. The only way to help these brave privileged men and women is by prayer. Persecution may drive them undergound, but man cannot kill the new life which is in them. Men can only stifle it. To them it is given, not only to believe in Christ's name, but also to suffer for his sake. What a glorious crown will be theirs when the Lord returns!

Throughout the world today God is working among Muslims. As one means of reaching them fails, we must find others. As doors close, we must be prepared to reach out to them, if not as full-time workers, then in other ways; and of these, the next chapter tells.

Chapter Fourteen

Youth Faces The Challenge Today

'Sir, we are delighted to know that Algerian Christians will be given the same liberty as Muslims in the new Algeria. Does this also mean that a Muslim will be free to change his faith and become a Christian?' asked a veteran French missionary.

'Such a thing is unthinkable,' was the unequivocal reply from the high Muslim official. To Muslims it is not only impossible that one of their faith should become Christian, but it is beyond the wildest bounds of imagination. Yet God is Almighty, and these men soon found to their consternation that young Algerians were turning to Christ. They were therefore compelled to restrict the promised liberty. Theoretically Islam grants freedom of worship, yet every Muslim knows that Islam is maintained and propogated by force. If this were not so there would be a mass movement from Islam to Christ.

The opposition in North Africa is three-fold. The family of the convert is violently opposed because the Christian has brought disgrace on them. They will employ ridicule, threats, physical pain, drugs, the occult and even poison to make the believer recant and turn from his Lord. The civil authorities continually track down a Christian. He is repeatedly called to appear before the police, suffers long periods of interrogation, is threatened and sometimes ill-treated.

Islam is not merely a religion. It is a culture, a way of life, a community, and the convert to Christianity is regarded by the civil authorities as suspect because he is a traitor to his country. Obviously the religious authorities are opposed, for to them Islam is the last and greatest religion and they will seek to maintain this theory by every means in their power. But in spite of this three-fold opposition, Muslims continued to turn to the Lord Jesus in Algeria, and in the post-war years there were probably more conversions and more baptisms than ever before.

A fair number of Christian men and women of various nationalities and from all walks of life continue to serve God while earning their living in a variety of professions; but to an ever increasing extent the gospel witness must be maintained by the national believers. These courageous men and women continue to render faithful service to God throughout North Africa. It was my privilege recently to attend one of their gatherings. The subject chosen for the two days of teaching was the Church of Christ in its three-fold aspect as a Body, a Building and a Bride. Messages were given by national believers, who evidenced true spiritual gifts. Both the classical Arabic Bible and the colloquial version were used for reading and study, and the messages were given in the colloquial. The singing was excellent and accompanied by guitars. The fifty Christians divided into five groups for Bible study and each group was led by a young believer who afterwards gave a short summary of their findings, girls as well as men taking part in this. All joined in the prayer meeting. Plans for future gatherings were in the hands of the national believers. Several of these evidenced the initiative and gift of leaders. It is obvious that an autonomous church exists, even though opposition and persecution may force it underground. To be a Christian in a Muslim land will always involve suffering, and it was a joy to meet a brother in the Lord who had just been released from prison. He had been condemned by a civil court because he had dared to break the Fast of Ramadhan.

God in his wisdom and grace foresaw the closing doors for the evangelisation of North Africa and has brought at least eight million Muslims to reside in Europe. In France alone it is estimated that there are at least one million and a half Muslims. Many are students with open minds and a real desire to be liberated from the bondage of Islam. Others are working in the mines and in factories or on building sites. They are beyond the reach of the jurisdiction of Muslim governments. Their religious leaders still do their utmost to prevent them from coming under the power of the gospel message, and their fellow countrymen still oppose, but they constitute a challenge to every keen young Christian. Efforts to reach them fall into three categories of which the most important is

Messages by Radio

These are beamed to North Africa from Monte Carlo by Trans-World Radio on the 25, 31 and 49 metres (short wave) and on the 205 medium wave bands. They comprise more than thirty messages a week in Arabic, one in Chleuh and two in Kabyle. Since this book records work among these fascinating people, it will be best if we confine our remarks to this last language, while remembering a yet more extensive work is carried on in Arabic.

Islam has always been the religion of the sword. When the Muslims conquered North Africa in the seventh century they found many established Christian churches. They destroyed the churches and attempted to impose their language and their religion on the entire population by force. Christianity had flourished among the Berber population. Augustine of Hippo was a Berber. It is the policy of the present Algerian Government to eliminate the Kabyle language and to replace it by Arabic. Kabyle children are taught Arabic in the day schools. All official broadcasts are in Arabic. Broadcasts in Kabyle have been banned and to some extent it is a forbidden language. The Berbers have never really been conquered and have always retained their language. Successive invasions by Arabs, Turks and French have all failed to conquer this virile race, or to eliminate their language. The Kabyles have reacted strongly to this attempt to exterminate them as a separate race, and have in turn made an effort to take all Arabic words from their vocabulary. They now call themselves *Imaziren,* and their language Thamazirth. They have adapted the script which was in use three thousand years ago in North Africa, and today in Paris is a centre where people are taught to read this new script. The movement is largely political and for this reason the new script cannot be employed for Kabyle publications. A certain Lalla Wardia has made use of this desire of over three million people to retain their own language, and she gives messages in Thamazirth which are followed increasingly by Kabyles in France and in Algeria. The speaker is so fluent that listeners are perplexed, not knowing if she herself is Kabyle, and the messages are so relevant that thousands are intrigued and listen in regularly. The following extracts from letters show the value of this work:

'Madame, your broadcasts every Tuesday and Saturday have made a great impression on my mind. I look forward to them each week. I should very much like to help you, for I have a large group of friends who want to know, who want to turn from their sins and be saved. Please try and understand me. I have taken up the cross and I will not be afraid. Excuse me for calling you Madame, for I do not know if you are a saint or not! Please send your reply by registered post.'

'Thanks for the book you sent me. I am so glad that

you continue the broadcasts in Kabyle. It is the best language for reaching our brothers in the mountains, and there are hundreds of them who listen. I should like to continue the Bible studies in Kabyle. Thank you so much for it is thanks to you and God that I am saved. I praise God that he opened my eyes to follow the right way, to know the Bible and to carry it out in my life.

Thanks to you I have discovered a new life, peace and joy. That is just what we are looking for. Please continue to send the lessons and your courses for I am much attached to you. Without you I should never have known the happiness I have found in Jesus Christ.'

The letters are not always complimentary as this letter shows:

'Dear Monkeys, having heard of your monkey tricks on the radio of November 13th, I feel that I should write and say this, "Your Christianity has not had the slightest effect on me. I don't practice any religion, not even Islam, the most important religion. You are a lot of hypocrites, good-for-nothing wild monkeys, who have escaped from their cages because they have not enough bananas to eat. If you think yourselves the most intelligent people, permit me to inform you that your intelligence is no better than that of a toad, who has very little brain. I am a revolutionary Algerian, a pure blooded Muslim, and all your medley is distasteful to me. If you have a reply you can send it over the radio.'

Needless to say, the letter was not answered over the radio, but the dear man listened, hundreds prayed for him in faith, and after a few months the following letter came from the same man:

I am writing to ask your forgiveness for all that I have written in the past against the Lord Jesus. I have finished my military service and am again free, I should so much like to follow a Bible correspondence course.

The letters received run into hundreds, and are from all sections of society, ranging from University students to 'shut-in' women.

Astonishing, sublime, extraordinary—to hear my language on radio!! I was absolutely stunned to hear Kabyle coming over the air in France!! I'm seeking a liberty I cannot find, though as a Berber I am a free man. I listen to your programmes continually, and have told many of my friends about them. They too are listening. It gives us Kabyles tremendous pleasure to listen to our language. Please send me literature, for I want to discover new horizons. I have a deep hunger to know the liberty of which you speak.

The Distribution of Literature and Contacts by Teams in Europe

During the summer of 1977 Operation Mobilisation made a special effort to reach Muslims in Europe. 1,500 keen young Christians formed teams which worked in France, Germany, England, Belgium, Austria, Spain, Turkey and other European countries. They used cassettes in Arabic, Turkish and Kabyle; sold packets of gospel literature suitable for all ages, gave records to those who had the facilities for listening, and sold New Testaments, Bibles and books.

At the invitation of OM leaders I was able to visit five teams in France during July, and three others in August. My experiences can but illustrate a very small part of the far-reaching campaign. The first week of each month was spent in conference in Belgium, when intensive teaching was given on Islam and the approach to Muslims. One text book that was used was *Share your faith with a Muslim,* Moody Press (the French edition is *Le Muslman mon prochain,* Telos). Muslims who live and work in Europe tend to group in the same towns, so that the first essential is to find the agglomerations of Kabyles, Algerians, Moroccans, or Turks. A good knowledge of their tribal language or dialect immediately opens doors. This is impossible for the short-time worker, but knowing their origin enables overseas workers to offer the correct books and cassettes.

In Roubaix the team leader made contact with the owner of a coffee house, and suggested that a small team should project Kodachromes depicting a story from Pakistan with an Arabic commentary. A team of four went in. Between thirty and forty men were gambling, smoking, playing cards and dominoes, and drinking, shouting and swearing. The din was indescribable. A less congenial audience for a gospel meeting could not be imagined. A Christian Arab from Jordan worked the projector. As soon as it was set up and the screen was in place, the leader said, 'It's up to you now, Charles, to invite them to come.' My heart quaked. How would they react? I started, '*Selam walikum* (Peace be on you)! We thought that you might be interested in seeing some pictures of Pakistan, and listening to the speaker who is an Arab. It is free for all who would like to come. Some of you, of course would prefer to go on playing. Might I suggest that as we shall be talking about God, you moderate your voices so that others can listen to the speaker. Thank you, and "Welcome" to you all.' Their reaction was startling. They looked at each other for a moment, and then every man in the café came across to listen, and most of them sat through until the end. Then I asked their permission to read to them the Word of God in Arabic. For a quarter of an hour I gave a simple direct gospel message. The usual questions followed, the atmosphere was extremely friendly, and we distributed tracts and sold some books and cassettes.

At Mulhouse we visited three lodging houses where single men can rent a bed, and meals are provided. This time we used a film 'Lost in the night.' It depicts in a graphic way the story of the lost sheep and the Good Shepherd. The setting was unfortunately Kenya, but the commentary was in the Arabic of North Africa. In one centre over one hundred men gathered and listened quietly until the end of the film. I followed on with a message in Arabic. There was some discussion, interesting questions were asked, and individual contacts made. 'What will you have to drink?' asked the barman. 'Your drinks are on the house. It is our way of saying "Thank you" for coming to us.'

At Lens contact was much more difficult, the reason being that the men did not know Arabic and I did not know their dialect of Berber. The very obvious lesson is that any who want to devote themselves to full-time work among Muslims in Europe must make an effort to speak the dialect of that particular group. Otherwise the contact is by literature or by using French.

When in Gibraltar I again went down to a huge lodging house, where nearly a thousand men slept in dormitories of sixty. The Muslim manager invited us to his room, men flocked in and when it was full, he bolted the door. The men invited me to read from the Bible. The next day six men visited the ship Logos and again I was asked to speak to them. They refused to leave without a message from the Bible. This then is the pattern for work in Europe. Distribute literature, make contacts, win their friendship and invite them to a centre—a private home or a room or coffee bar attached to a church. Muslims have an almost uncanny knack of discerning those who are transparently sincere and who really love them. Among those who had this love for Muslims were a Swede, an American and a Frenchman. Each of these easily made contacts, and won the confidence of the Muslims. I followed up the contacts and had the joy of leading several Muslims to Christ. I was just a link in the chain. The initial contacts were made by others with a very superficial knowledge of the language. The task of the girls was more difficult. Several made good contacts with women when the man of the house was out at work, and succeeded in getting into homes. When they returned on the Saturday or Sunday to follow up the contacts and the man of the house was there, the Arabs would not even open the door. Nevertheless, some did and there were several professions of conversion among the women and these appeared to be genuine.

With each cassette, record, packet of booklets or New Testament was an invitation to follow a correspondence course. The following letter indicates that such work is not without fruit:

It is 2:20 a.m. as I write to you. I am a young man of 18, and my reason for writing is that I have been listening to your cassette 'Worthwhile Fruit', and I find it just 'Super', especially on the subject of religion. I'm so glad that I am not the only one to believe in Jesus Christ, for even before listening to your cassette I did not believe in Islam. Islam is for the Arabs and not for Kabyles. I believe in God Almighty and in Jesus Christ. Our religion today is, as it always has been—The Cross.

The Individual and Collective Witness of Converted Muslims

It would be unwise to disclose their location or their methods, but there is little doubt that converted Muslims are keen, devoted men and God is using them today. Some are full time evangelists. Where it is possible for individuals and churches to co-operate with Christians from North Africa, results are achieved, but the mutual atmosphere of suspicion must be replaced by genuine, yet discerning friendship.

What then is the biggest hindrance to the evangelisation of Muslims? It has always been, and still is, just lack of faith. In the early days of our missionary work I told a Muslim of the love of the Lord Jesus, of his sacrifice for our sins, and of his power to save. He replied, 'What wonderful words! Are there many others besides yourself who know this?'

'Indeed there are.' I replied. 'There are millions in the world who have found forgiveness and peace and joy through faith in him.'

'But surely no one else in this land knows about Jesus Christ?'

'Oh yes, they do.'

'How many others know about him and his power to save?'

'There must be at least a hundred others like me in Algiers alone.'

'Then, if they really believe it, why has no one ever been to tell us here? No, you Christians do not really believe what you say. If you did really believe some one would have come to us before.' Thus, this Muslim youth, with wonderful acumen and insight, pinpointed the reason for the non-evangelisation of Muslims— Unbelief. 'You do not really believe or some one would have come to us long ago.' The words pierced my heart like a sword. That was fifty years ago, but in that small area known as Lesser Kabylia, Pearl and I were the only ones to attempt to tell the half a million unevangelised Muslims of our wonderful Lord. During those forty years when the doors were wide open, why had no one joined us? Why was I compelled to trudge the mountains alone? Why did Pearl plod on alone with open doors on every hand to speak to the shut-in women? Just one word. Unbelief. The paucity of spiritual results in Muslim work must in large measure be placed at the door of unbelieving Christians. 'He did not do many miracles there because of their lack of faith.' Islam defies your King. The challenge remains.

The background of this book has been Algeria, and when we first faced the challenge over fifty years ago there were eight million Muslims there. Today eight million Muslims have come to Europe! The door is still wide open. The challenge remains. Will you face it and give your life to this all-important task of reaching Muslims? Can you go in part time service to some Muslim land? Can you give two years of your life, or even a few months to join an outreach team? Islam still defies your King.

'I have set my King on Zion, my holy hill' (Ps. 2:6). That is God's reply to the challenge of Islam. 'Ask of me, and I will make the nations your inheritance, the ends of the earth your possession. You will rule them with an iron sceptre.' Man cannot, dare not challenge God in blatant unbelief. Jesus shall reign. Every knee must bow to him, but that will be in the day of judgement, the day of his power. Today God acts in sovereign grace as the following incident shows.

Sameena was born in Algeria of good Muslim parents. In her youth she went to Paris, and achieved some notoriety by writing poems on love and appearing on TV. She had a deep thirst to know God. It was not satisfied at the mosque, so she dressed as a European and attended Mass in a Roman Catholic church, but the deep longing to know Jesus Christ still remained. Returning to Algiers she became a reporter for a local Arabic newspaper. While on her way home one night in the company of an Algerian reporter for the same paper, he discovered through conversation that she was still a virgin, and took her to the side of the street and abused her. Arriving at her home, her brother opened the door, saw from the state of her clothes what had happened and rushed upstairs to get a carving knife. Had it not been for the timely intervention of her father, who wrenched the knife from his hand, he would have killed her there and then, and vindicated the honour of the family. Sameena had similar experiences with other Algerians. She was so disgusted and disillusioned with men who witnessed to God and yet abused pure girls that she left Algeria and went to Europe, ending up as an 'au pair' girl in London. She found this life rather tame and joined a party of hippies living in the East End of London. She was soon hooked on drugs. She married a young Englishman, also a drug addict, and they drifted to the West of England where they existed in a broken-down caravan. It was there that their baby was born. Funds were short, they stole powdered milk and nappies for the baby, but were soon arrested by the police. Sameena was so violent that they took her baby from her, and shut her in a padded cell. This was where God intervened in love and grace. Just as Saul of Tarsus had done years ago, she saw the Lord. The whole cell was filled with dazzling light. He spoke to Sameena and told her that he had redeemed her. He would set her free from the power of drugs and sin. When the wardress came the next morning and opened the cell door to conduct her before the judge, she said to her, *'Je suis libre. Jesus Christ m'a affranchi* (I am free. Jesus Christ has set me free). The judge can condemn me to whatever prison sentence he likes, but I have met Jesus Christ. I am free.' She was released, and shortly after that I met her and her husband. Later I visited them in their home on several occasions. She led her husband to the Lord, they were baptised and brought into the fellowship of a local church. On one occasion it was a joy to spend the whole day with them and to hear the tragic story with the wonderful climax. She is one of the many Muslims, both men and women, who have been saved through the direct intervention of a triumphant Lord.

It would appear to many that Satan has triumphed through the expulsion of full-time workers from Algeria and other Muslim lands; but even as I write these lines, very evident proof has come from several independent sources that God is working in those lands as never before. It is impossible to defeat the Living God. His power is infinite, his ways past understanding, and his work continues. In his grace he still reveals his Son to Muslims and no one can stop him. In his grace he still asks you to face the challenge of Islam. Will you? Now?

Chapter Fifteen

The Challenge to You

This final chapter brings the challenge to you, a committed Christian, jealous for the honour of your Lord, longing that Muslims should experience the thrill of finding new life in Christ. At the beginning of this book you read of how we were turned out of our first home, and faced the bleak prospect of living in the Arab village of Hammam.

'You will never succeed in winning those people. They are the most bigoted and fanatical Muslims of the whole district. More than that, you don't even know their language. Your task is hopeless.' Anna was one of our closest friends. She knew well the people of the whole district where she had been born. A practising Protestant, she had been instrumental in obtaining for us our first home at Lafayette. Thirty years later, when the civil war was at its height and Europeans were being killed every day on the streets of Lafayette (yet when hundreds of Muslims were still coming to us at the Hammam) I reminded Anna of her words. She replied, 'Yes, I was sure that it was an impossible task, but you found the way to win their friendship and confidence through love. In spite of the bitter feelings brought on by war they still trust you.'

As we look out on the world today we cannot avoid realising the political aspect of the Muslim situation. We are saddened at the intense suffering brought to many by Islam in other lands. Although committed to Christ as Lord, and loving the Muslim wherever he may be found, we are still intelligent men and women. Through the media we are in touch with the facts of the world situation, and the challenge of an immigrant population must not blind us to them. The presentation of Islam as a wonderful culture must not obscure the realities of missionaries expelled from Muslim lands, of bloodshed and strife, of mass executions. But the love of Christ controls us because we are convinced that One has died for all—including the Muslims who are now our guests and our neighbours. His love must be the controlling factor.

Muslims are convinced that their religion is right. Therefore they practise what they believe and propagate their faith. They plan to visit every house in Britain with Islamic propaganda, and to place a mosque in every sizeable town. They use the media to give an attractive picture of Islam and seek to discredit Christianity through literature. Sweden is predicted to be won for Islam before the turn of the century. If Muslims avail themselves of the freedom of our Western civilisation which allows them to propagate their faith, surely we Christians must avail ourselves of our right to witness to our living Lord. We cannot all go abroad to reach Muslims, nor would they allow us to enter their lands, but we can make friendly contacts here.

At first sight it would seem that this wonderful opportunity to evangelise Muslims is here on our doorstep. Muslims can now have the same privilege of hearing the message of life and responding to it as any other person residing in the United Kingdom. But the keen Christian who endeavours to contact Muslims is confronted with many problems. The immigrant has been warned against those who will seek to turn him from his faith. He is already prejudiced by the teaching that he has received since childhood concerning the Christian faith. His grasp of English is slight. He misunderstands many religious terms. Women often speak no English at all. Fear and suspicion keep him from breaking in any way from the local community of Islam. Any contact with Christians will probably be met with threats from his own people coupled with warnings of the dangers of becoming involved. A Muslim who has only once been approached by a Christian may find that in various ways drugs and even the occult are being used by his own people to deter him from following up the contact. Read again chapter five of this book. Even in Britain, Islam refuses the Muslim the liberty to hear God's Word and to follow his conscience. Who then are the Muslims with whom contact may be made?

Students in Colleges and Universities. These are the people who are most open and accessible. They rub shoulders in college with Christian students. They have been trained to think for themselves. They are deeply conscious of the limitations of Islam, of the restrictions placed on them by the Fast and the regular times of prayer. Some may even deny the existence of God. While the younger generation is much more open, it must be remembered that they are controlled by the older generation which is much more conservative. Most students are here on grants, they are closely watched by religious authorities moving on the campus. They are not completely free. Yet in many universities and colleges friendly contacts can be made and maintained during the limited period that the student is in Britain.

Quite recently I was invited to speak to the students of the Christian Union on the campus of a university. The gathering was planned for Saturday evening. Muslim students expressed their interest and said that if we could have a meeting especially for them, the Islamic Society would turn up in full force. We arranged a special gathering on the Sunday afternoon. Nearly thirty men from many countries were present. I announced the subject: 'Who is Jesus Christ?' and asked to be allowed to develop it for forty minutes. Then they were to feel perfectly free to ask questions. We informed them that we did not want a debate on comparative religions. As we look round the world today we see that religion divides, and creates bitterness. We wanted to remain friends and to come to a better understanding of each other. A chairman was chosen; the discussion was rather heated at times during the two-hour period, but the situation was always under control. At the end, tea and coffee were provided, and the friendly discussion continued. I had to leave to conduct the evening service at the local church. To my surprise four of these Muslims found their way to the church. I was delighted to see them. The message was not aimed at them. It was the simple gospel, and at times the men openly expressed their approval. Later, church members chatted with them. It was evident that they felt quite at home and three remained for the after-church gathering when slides of North Africa were shown. All this was made possible by the friendly attitude of the students, and the co-operation of the pastor and church members—not by my one short visit.

Business Men. Here contact is possible on a different level. These men are usually astute, ready to drive a hard bargain; and uppermost in their minds is the thought that business is business. But—they need Christ, and must be reached.

Workmates. They observe you at every moment of the day. Be friendly, avoid giving undue offence, and at the appropriate time invite the man to have coffee in your home. You may then be invited to visit him, and you will need to be very discreet. It is advisable to invite one person at the time. If more come, you must be much more guarded.

Neighbours. The possibilities of friendly contacts are tremendous, but again fraught with difficulties. Where newly arrived immigrants are concerned, the first approach should *never* be along the line of religion or a direct witness to Christ. A friendly smile between ladies, a word of advice regarding the best shops to frequent and suitable clothing for our changeable climate, are good ice-breakers. Often it is through the children that contact can be made. And sometimes in England an official form must be filled out by those who have a very superficial knowledge of English and your help would be valued. You could even offer your help in writing an English letter.

As almost the entire population of a Muslim land is Muslim, they are convinced that every Englishman is a Christian, and Christianity is judged on this basis. False impressions are formed. In Algeria a distinction is made between Europeans (who may be nominal Christians) and true believers. The first are called *nasara* and the others *imasihiyin*. If an Algerian national were asked if I and my family were *nasara* he would immediately say, 'No, you are *imasihiyin*—you are true believers, the people of the Book.' How did he know the difference? It was through years of personal friendship, by sharing on the person-to-person level, through love in action in so many small ways. Gradually we won their confidence, and were finally regarded as one of them. We spoke with them of answers to prayer that we had received. They saw many healed through treatment at the clinic. Friendly advice was offered on many subjects. We quoted promises from the Bible assuring us of God's presence and protection, and they saw that he did protect us. He was with us. They began to ask serious questions, and when anyone asks a question all the tension goes out of witnessing.

Conditions in Britain are vastly different, but the principle is the same. Love will always find a way. The situation may seem hopeless to you. So it did to us at first, but love found ways to get through with our message. So do not attempt to witness or to lead a Muslim to Christ until you have established your right to speak of the things of God. His first impression is that you are a *kafer*, a heathen, an idolater. What right has a heathen to teach a Muslim, a believer, about God? Reverse the position. If he as a Muslim began to teach you, a committed Christian, about God, would you be inclined to listen to him? So why should he listen to you? Therefore, your first concern must be to establish the fact that you do know God, that you are a believer. You must try and understand him and his culture, not as it is presented ideally by the BBC, but as he is really in daily life. Bear in mind these six points:

He is a Muslim from birth, one who professes to be wholly surrendered to God, to accept the will of Allah without questioning. He is a fatalist, and all that happens to him is by the will of God. He has no choice. Man is like a bird in a cage which is carried by its owner wherever he wills. The bird may struggle or remain quiet. It makes no difference. If a man sins it is because God willed it, otherwise he would have prevented him. If God wants him to be saved he will be. There is no need for him to make a personal decision. He bows before God in prayer because he is the slave and God his Master. God decides. However, even though he may deny it, deep in the heart of every Muslim is a fear of God. He must meet God on the day of judgement. God exists and is all-powerful. This is your point of contact—the fear of God.

He is a traditionalist. He may know all the 'answers' to Christianity, having heard them since he was a boy. The first chapter of the Koran that he learned is *Sura 112*. 'Say he is Allah, he neither begets nor is he begotten.' Or again concerning the Lord Jesus, 'He was not killed, he was not crucified, it only seemed so to them' (*Sura 4:158*). So he will start with these verses and attack your faith. He is sure that his traditions based on the Koran are unanswerable. By attacking what you believe he puts you on the defensive. If you take the initiative and approach him along another line he is lost for an answer, and is immediately out of his depth.

He is the prisoner of his environment. Being Muslim he is a member of a world-wide community and must conform. Islam is more than a religion. It is also a culture, a way of life, and for him to break with this is to become a traitor to his country and his people. It is important for the Christian to realise this. In our countries a man is free to decide, to think for himself, to follow his conscience, and to accept the faith that he chooses, but in Islam this is impossible. In becoming a Christian he renounces his religion, his family, his friends and his country. He is rejected by one community and not yet accepted by the other. It is wise therefore to avoid exerting any pressure on him, and to allow the Holy Spirit to work. Remember the high price that a Muslim pays when he breaks with Islam. Many think that baptism should be postponed until several can take the step together. Read chapter five again. In many ways it applies here.

He is a believer; not a Christian, but he sincerely believes in God, in his angels and evil spirits, the Scriptures or revealed books, his messengers and prophets, the day of resurrection, and heaven and hell. Although most of his beliefs are distorted and false they serve as a base of contact. He knows the histories of many of the prophets of the Old Testament. He believes that Jesus is the Word of God and the Son of Mary. He knows that Christ will return to this earth. All this makes it possible to apply the principle which is at the base of all teaching. Start with what he knows and lead him on to a full and correct faith. He knows that God is light and in him is no darkness at all. Congratulate him on this, and using the Bible teach him what he does not know. His conscience will tell him that God's Word, from which you read, is right and true.

He is frank and open in stating what he believes, and

will admire anyone who has the courage to state clearly his faith. For instance you can say, 'Every believer has three enemies. The first is the devil, the second the world—what is the third?' He may place his hand over his heart, and say 'His evil nature, himself.' 'Which is the greatest enemy?' 'The greatest is his heart, for it never leaves him.' Now you read to him Romans 7:18-24. You have approached him as a believer, and he usually responds favourably.

He is a sinner for whom Christ died. Deep down in his heart he longs for forgiveness. Many times a day he repeats the phrase, *'Esteghofer Allah* (I ask pardon of God)'—yet in Islam he can only *hope* to be forgiven. Only through the Lord Jesus can he have the *assurance* of sins forgiven. As we look into his face we must remember that he is a man whom our Saviour loves, for whom he died, and try and forget that he is a Muslim. He needs forgiveness for the past, strength to overcome for the present and hope for the future. This is our message and because he is conscious that he is a sinner he will sometimes respond.

He is human and will respond to kindness and affection. It is not possible to tell him that God loves him, for he misunderstands love. (John 3:16 is the *last* verse to read to a Muslim.) Yet in his innermost being he is looking for someone whom he can trust, someone who cares about him, who will not let him down. This is why we try not to offend him by attacking his religion or discrediting the character of his prophet. We endeavour to avoid controversy. When in his country, and to some extent here, we try as far as possible to adapt ourselves to his culture. Most of them know instinctively someone who loves them, someone who really cares. We show it in so many ways. Remain friendly in times of political tension, and never fail to greet them with *'Selam oualikoum!'* We show sympathy during an illness or at times of bereavement. If unavoidably drawn into a discussion which becomes heated, we must never fail to return the next day, not to preach, or to renew the argument, but to show him that we still remain friendly in spite of the bitter things he has said to us. In these and so many other ways we show him that we love him, and that we really care, not just for his soul, but for him.

Mistakes to avoid

Do not give him free tuition on Islam! Remember that not every Muslim is a theologian. In fact, many who come to Europe as students or workmen know very little about their faith. A man in the villages of Algeria once assured me, 'Everything I know about Islam I have learned from missionaries!' The Christian states 'The Bible says . . ., but you Muslims believe . . .' The Muslim was totally unaware of that particular point of the Islamic faith. It was the missionary who taught him. Avoid the type of discussion which is based on comparative religion. Religions have always antagonised, but faith in a living God who works in men's lives carries conviction.

Don't go against his culture. If you invite him to a meal, please do not offer him ham sandwiches or bacon and eggs.

In some Islamic communities, you should never admire the baby, especially if you are a single girl.

In work among Muslims, men go to men, and women to women. If a young lady approaches a young man with a smile and offers him a tract, he can only interpret it in one way. Such things are not done in the world of Islam except by fast women. The intentions of the girl may be good, but she is in danger. More converts are won for Islam today in England through girls falling in love with Muslims and marrying them than in any other way. The results can be disastrous.

God Meets the Challenge

Five times a day from ten thousand minarets throughout the world the words *Allah Akbar* (God is greater) ring out. Every Muslim, every Christian, would agree to that. God will have, he *must* have, the last word. It is only in a secondary sense that a man makes Jesus King when he yields to him the throne of his life and allows him full control. Yet you may still defy him and state dogmatically that Islam defies him. 'He who sits in the heavens laughs; the Lord has them in derision. Then he will speak to them in his wrath, and terrify them in his fury saying, *"I have set my King on Zion, my holy hill."* I will tell of the decree of the Lord' (Psalm 2:4-7).

When we turn to the New Testament we are left in no doubt that this King is Jesus Christ. 'He humbled himself and became obedient unto death—even death on a cross! Therefore God has highly exalted him and bestowed on him the name which is above every name, that at the name of Jesus every knee should bow . . . and every tongue confess that Jesus Christ is Lord, to the glory of God the Father' (Phil. 2:8-11). 'He must reign until he has put all his enemies under his feet' (1 Cor. 15:5). 'When the Son of Man comes in his glory . . . he will sit on his throne in heavenly glory. All the nations will be gathered before him' (Matt. 25:31,32).

Scriptures such as these could be multiplied to show just how clearly God has met and will meed this defiant challenge of Islam. The Lord Jesus will return to reign, and men will be divided by him into two classes; those who have bowed to him in obedience and worship, and those who rebel. Men mocked his title when they nailed him to the Cross; 'This is Jesus, the King of the Jews.'

Some still rebel and refuse to own his supremacy. Have you bowed to him? Is he *your* Lord, your King? There is still time in this day of grace to bow and find in him new life. Then you will face the proud defiant challenge and join with us in taking the message of reconcilation to those who still rebel. God has met the challenge and he is greater than men. He has declared:

I have set my King on Zion, my holy hill

The decree has gone out, and God will honour his Word. Blessed are all they that put their trust in him.